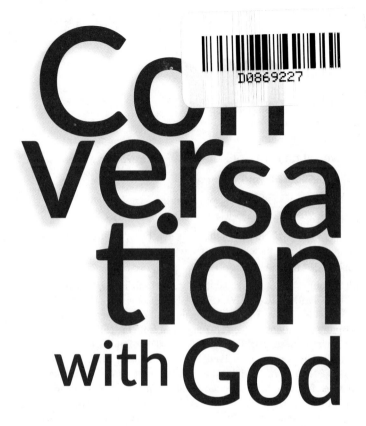

Conversation with God

The Power of Prevailing Prayer

Brian T. Sutton

BroadStreet
PUBLISHING

BroadStreet Publishing Group, LLC
Racine, Wisconsin, USA
BroadStreetPublishing.com

Conversation with God: *The Power of Prevailing Prayer*

Copyright © 2017 Brian T. Sutton

ISBN-13: 978-1-4245-5554-3 (softcover)
ISBN-13: 978-1-4245-5555-0 (e-book)

All Scriptures, unless marked otherwise, are from THE HOLY BIBLE, NEW INTERNATIONAL VERSION®, NIV® Copyright © 1973, 1978, 1984, 2011 by Biblica, Inc.® Used by permission. All rights reserved worldwide. Scripture quotations marked NLT are taken from the Holy Bible, New Living Translation, copyright © 1996, 2004, 2007 by Tyndale House Foundation. Used by permission of Tyndale House Publishers, Inc., Carol Stream, Illinois 60188, USA. All rights reserved. Scripture quotations marked NASB are taken from the *New American Standard Bible*, © Copyright 1960, 1962, 1963, 1968, 1971, 1972, 1973, 1975, 1977 by The Lockman Foundation. Used by permission. Scripture marked KJV is taken from the King James Version of the Bible. Public Domain.

Emphases in Scripture quotations are those of the author.

Stock or custom editions of BroadStreet Publishing titles may be purchased in bulk for educational, business, ministry, fundraising, or sales promotional use. For information, please e-mail info@broadstreetpublishing.com.

Cover design by Chris Garborg at garborgdesign.com
Interior design and typesetting by Katherine Lloyd at theDESKonline.com

Printed in the United States of America

17 18 19 20 21 5 4 3 2 1

This work is dedicated to my late brother, William Jason Sutton. He left this life on January 9, 2015. Jason was quite possibly the funniest person I've ever known. I can easily close my eyes and see him gushing with a loud laugh as he slapped his leg. His heart was drawn to those who were downtrodden and cast away by others. May we all strive to live in the love of Jesus that reaches to the "least of these" around us.

Contents

Foreword

I t does not necessarily concern satan when the church announces a board meeting, a leadership conference, or another spectacular event. He has repeatedly watched these happen without doing much harm to his work on the earth. However, when satan hears that the church is going to develop a lifestyle of conversation with God through prevailing prayer, he knows that we are engaging in a realm of power that causes him and his imps to tremble. Through the power of prayer, satan has been defeated in every confrontation, beginning when he was an archangel who challenged the rule of God.

Unfortunately, among many Christians today, prayer is more assumed than achieved; it is more preached than practiced. Prayer is too often reserved for crises, rather than done in the sphere of everyday life. Many churches today have been duped into believing that plans, programs, organizations, personal skills, or charisma may be substituted for prayer. Not so! There is no substitute for prayer.

Brian Sutton is perfectly clear in his call for prevailing prayer. To *prevail* means to prove superior in strength, power, or influence. In this matter, Pastor Sutton is in full agreement with the apostle Paul who said in 2 Corinthians 2:5, "we are not sufficient of ourselves to think any thing as of ourselves; but our sufficiency is of God" (KJV).

Acknowledging our irrefutable human deficiencies through prevailing prayer, we call upon the strength, power, and influence of the one who said that "this battle is not yours, but mine." Jesus Christ, our Advocate, made it possible for us to "come boldly unto the throne of grace, that we may obtain mercy, and find grace to help in time of need" (Hebrews 4:16 KJV).

In this book, Pastor Sutton does not present warmed-over clichés regarding prayer but probes deeply into the biblical definition of prayer, with special emphasis on how Jesus taught his disciples that prayer was more than an event—it was entering a conversation with God. Is it possible that these Jewish men whom Christ chose as disciples did not know how to pray? Not hardly. Their Jewish faith taught them to pray at least five times a day. But they wanted to know Jesus' way of praying.

Jesus' way of praying was so much more personal than what they had been taught by the rabbis. Jesus' way of praying sounded more like a child having an intimate conversation with his father, and the disciples could relate to that. Interestingly, the disciples never asked Jesus to teach them to preach, teach, or lead, but they asked him to teach them to pray. Jesus taught them that prayer was to be perpetual and ongoing communication with God.

Multiple hours are spent in teaching Christians many things, but little to no time is spent teaching us how to communicate with God. Pastor Sutton makes an extraordinary appeal to correct that. My hope and prayer is that we will take notice.

Conversation with God: The Power of Prevailing Prayer focuses on prayer as communication. Communication is a two-way street. In prayer, we not only speak to God, but we endeavor to hear God speak. Scripture tells us in Exodus 33:11, "And the LORD spake unto Moses face to face, as a man speaketh unto his friend" (KJV). How incredible is that? We are in a relationship with God that involves give and take. The act of sincere prayer emboldens us to see ourselves as God sees us—as sons and daughters, members of his family who are privileged to have regular conversation with our Father. Prayer is a natural outcome of our relationship with God.

Let us never forget that it is not good works that God honors; it is a relationship. It is prayer, not good works, that drive toward a rightful relationship with God and with fellow humans. The casualties of the spiritual life may be traced back to the point of one's failure to establish effective communication with God through prevailing prayer.

Our culture has so filled our ears with the excess of human noises that the voice of God is too often obscured. So much of life is so artificial that we attempt to cover it with entertainment and special effects. How much longer can we stay in touch with the inner-spirit when the demons of our busy world are making so much noise? The answer lies in the theme of this book. God desires us to move beyond mere survival and artificial living. He is calling us to an overcoming and victorious life through prayer.

The highest achievement of the Christian life is prayer and conversation with God, because it means that we are in God's company and in union with him. Unquestionably, this is greatly illustrated by Pastor Sutton when he calls for a lifestyle of conversation with God. Although he emphasizes the importance of specific acts of prayer, he reminds us that, above all else, prayer is the desire for God, and that is much more than a programmed event.

The personal experiences of Pastor Sutton relating to the power of prayer and its impact on his life add an indisputable value to this book. He shares examples of family and others who have influenced his prayer life, which provides us with great insight as to why Pastor Sutton is so committed to this vital subject. It is my sincere hope and prayer that this book will bring each of us into a dramatic awakening of the spiritual life through fervent, effectual, and persistent prayer.

Lamar Vest
Former President and CEO of American Bible Society

How to
Use This Resource

Do you ever wish for more closeness in your relationship with Jesus? *Conversation with God* is a perfect resource for personal and small-group study. Do you ever long to see God's people ministering to the Lord in first-century power? *Conversation with God* can be effectively used as a church-wide devotional guide. Do you ever sense a burden to see a reclaiming of God's church as a house of prayer? *Conversation with God* is ideal for prayer summits, prayer retreats, pastoral prayer teams, or beginning an intercessory prayer ministry.

Conversation with God is unique. It is unlike any of the resources you've likely read before, because the exercises in each chapter were written with the specific goal of engaging you in conversations with God. These exercises were created to move you beyond seeking to simply know about God to moving toward experiencing and relating to him. Why is this important? Because it's only an experiential, Spirit-empowered faith that can live out our ultimate calling. The *Conversation with God* resource is designed to foster this kind of faith.

Conversation with God has a specific focus on ministering to the Lord through more deeply loving him with all our heart, mind, soul, and strength (see Acts 13:2; Matthew 22:37). The ultimate goal of our faith journey is not acquiring more facts or learning more doctrine; our faith is about a person. It's this relational perspective on loving the Lord that produces Christlikeness and a faith that is marked by the Spirit's power.

Ten specific "Loving the Lord" discipleship outcomes are listed and fully described in the Appendices of this resource. Within the text, these outcomes are labeled as L1–L10. You'll find the outcomes within the devotional exercises throughout *Conversation with God*. (An entire framework for spiritual growth has been drawn from a cluster analysis of several Greek and Hebrew words that declare that Christ's followers are to be equipped for works of ministry or service. See the Appendices.)

Next, imagine this: You've just begun a journey. It's as if you're going for a walk. As you read through *Conversation with God*, we invite you to walk in the light of God's Son (see John 8:12), in the light of God's Word (see Psalm 119:105), and in the light of God's people (see Matthew 5:14). The devotional exercises contained in this resource are designed around these three sources of light. When you come to an exercise, we recommend that you pause right then and have a conversation with God.

We're delighted that you've decided to take this walk with God. Be encouraged. God's Word reminds us that it's vitally important to walk in the light. In fact, Jesus told his disciples, "Walk while you have the light" (John 12:35).

The Great Commandment Network has developed the devotional exercises in this resource, the Spirit-empowered discipleship framework, and, in collaboration with others, the Spirit-empowered outcomes that are included. The Great Commandment Network's deepest desire it to serve our friend, Brian Sutton, and the cause of Spirit-empowered discipleship.

The Great Commandment Network is an international collaborative network of strategic, kingdom leaders from the faith community, marketplace, education, and caregiving fields who prioritize the powerful simplicity of the words of Jesus to love God, live his Word, love people, and live his mission.

Chapter 1

Prayer Is Conversation
with God

My grandfather, Paul Sutton, was not a preacher; he was a farmer, but he taught me much about God. He wore denim overalls practically every day, other than on Sundays when he went to church. I learned much about prayer as conversation with God from listening to my grandfather pray.

I was one of many grandchildren in the Sutton family, sixteen, to be exact. At one time, many of us attended the same church in rural Lawrence County, Alabama. It was wonderful to be raised in that small church with a big family.

All the grandkids loved to spend the night at Granddaddy and Grandmother's house. It was a small, white house situated on a farm, but it miraculously swelled to accommodate all the grandchildren whenever we wanted to spend the night.

My grandmother, Beatrice, was a fantastic cook. We were often awakened in the morning by the smell of her biscuits, thick chocolate gravy (a Southern breakfast dish), and various meats being fried from the livestock Granddaddy raised. For me, those times spent with cousins at my grandparents' house were precious. They were grand for many reasons, but perhaps the grandest of reasons was the opportunity I had to listen to Granddaddy pray.

Every night at bedtime, Granddaddy would turn off the television, stop all activity, and gather all of us into the living room. He would then ask us to find a place to pray, and we would all kneel. Granddaddy's small living room would be filled with tiny Sutton kids on our knees beside Granddaddy and Grandmother. All ages were represented. We all said our dutiful prayers for our parents, siblings, Sunday school teachers, pets, football teams, "Bear" Bryant, or whatever else was on our young hearts. Eventually the room would grow still as our little voices faded off and got quiet. We'd slowly stop praying, one by one, and wander off to our beds. But whenever our prayers ceased, Granddaddy's didn't. He always continued to pray even after we were all finished.

He would talk to God like he was talking to his friend. And I distinctly remember one specific line from Granddaddy— I've never heard anyone say it quite like him—"Lord, bless all those that it is our duty to pray for." When we heard him pray, we knew Granddaddy was listening to God. But perhaps even more so, when we heard him pray, we knew God was listening to Granddaddy. It was a conversation between heaven and earth. Hearing Granddaddy's prayers helped me realize early on that prayer is simply a conversation with God. We speak and we listen. We talk and we hear. God wants us to converse with him, much like speaking with a friend.

Jeremiah 33:3 says, "Call to me and I will answer you and tell you great and unsearchable things you do not know." These are powerful words indeed—a promise from God. Why then would we *not* pray? The truth is that we have many reasons. And even when we pray, prayer can become just another option for us, something to pick up and put down for our own purposes. But it can and should be so much more than that.

The truth is that prayer is a mighty vehicle for us. It is something we use to carry out the purposes of God in our lives. We know prayer can increase the effectiveness of our ministry; we know prayer will boost our ability to reach the harvest. We pray so we can lead; we pray so we can work; and we pray so we can preach. We pray so we can accomplish what God wants us to accomplish. We pray so we can talk to God. And we pray so we can hear from God.

Prayer and the life of prayer are spiritual practices. I cannot explain them to you; rather, they must be experienced. I've seen a myriad of T-shirts and bumper stickers that say, "Prayer changes things." But prayer does not change things. Prayer has no power whatsoever in and of itself. If simply being enthusiastic about prayer as a powerful vehicle were enough, I could pray to anything and receive an answer. No, prayer doesn't change things; it is God who changes things! I'll say it again: It is not prayer or even a life of prayer that brings us power; it is the God to whom we pray who has all power.

Paul said in 1 Thessalonians 5:16–18, "Rejoice always, pray continually, give thanks in all circumstances; for this is God's will for you in Christ Jesus." The church has been called to pray continually. You and I have been called to pray continually, pray without stopping. It is a vital part of the life of a Christian. Whatever has gone on in the past, you can decide today that you're going to be a person who prays—a person who maintains a lifestyle of prayer. I've made the decision—I will pray.

It's not prayer itself that has the power; rather, it is the God we pray to who has the power.

MAKE THE DECISION:
AN EXPERIENCE OF SCRIPTURE

Jesus replied: "Love the Lord your God with all your heart and with all your soul and with all your mind." (Matthew 22:37)

Make the decision to pray by first learning to love God and making him your priority. Since the greatest of all the commandments is to love God, let's pause to consider the question: "How is it that we really love God?" Often our response indicates that we believe that loving God is equal to doing things *for* God. All the while, he is simply longing for us to *relate* to him.

If God needed something done, then he could enlist the angels for perfect execution and without complaint. We, as his created image bearers, have the privilege of intimacy with him. Our journey with God in prayer provides this unique opportunity.

As we approach him in prayer, where do we begin? The psalmist declares:

Worship the Lord with gladness;
    come before him with joyful songs.

Know that the LORD is God.
  It is he who made us, and we are his;
  we are his people, the sheep of his pasture.
Enter his gates with thanksgiving
  and his courts with praise;
  give thanks to him and praise his name.
(Psalm 100:2–4)

Imagine that you're a parent and one of your teenagers initiates this conversation: "Mom/Dad, I'd like to take this time to share the gratefulness I feel for all the ways you have loved me so well!" What an absolute miracle that would be, right? But wouldn't you agree that kind of heartfelt expression of gratitude communicates love? Likewise, you and I express our love to the Lord in many relational ways, and one of the most important is through our gratitude.

Prayer is a *journey* into deepened love with the Lord. "Rejoice always, pray continually, give thanks in all circumstances; for this is God's will for you in Christ Jesus" (1 Thessalonians 5:16–18). Pause now to pray a prayer of thanksgiving and serve God with a glad heart:

Father, as I reflect on the countless ways you have loved me well, my heart overflows with thanksgiving. I'm especially grateful for how you have blessed me with _____, and how you have sustained me through _____. I praise you for your generosity and grace. Receive my thanksgiving and praise as a small expression of my deep love. Amen.

SPIRIT-
EMPOWERED
Faith   **L1. *Practicing thanksgiving in all things.***

In 1 John 5:14, we read, "This is the confidence we have in approaching God: that if we ask anything according to his will, he hears us." Prayer is a conversation with the one who is always there. It allows us access through Jesus Christ into a conversation with God. The Father is always seeking a conversation with us; he greatly desires to communicate with us.

My wife, Renee, and I recently did some redecorating in our upstairs bathroom. We took down some wallpaper, spackled a few holes, and repainted the walls. She purchased some new decorations and pictures. Of course, she wanted me to hang these pictures on the walls.

So I went into my garage, reached into my black tool bag, pulled out my hammer, and grabbed some nails from my old plastic ice-cream bucket. I took my hammer and used it to drive in every one of those nails in the exact location where Renee wanted the pictures hung.

When I finished, I hung the pictures and headed back into my garage. I opened my black tool bag once again, placed my hammer back inside, and zipped up the bag. Finished! Right now, as I'm writing this, my hammer is put away. I know where it will be the next time I need to drive in a few nails or hang up more pictures. That's using my hammer as the tool for which it was intended.

We might as well admit it: We often use prayer in our lives and in the church as a tool from a tool bag. When we need God to do something for us, when we need something in ministry, when we desire to have something accomplished, we go to the spiritual tool bag because we know that prayer is what we should use. We pick up prayer, we pray the prayer, and then we put prayer back in the bag until we need it again. But prayer is intended to be so much more than this!

What if prayer was not simply a vehicle to take us somewhere? What if prayer was not just a tool to get God to move when we wanted him to? What if we could participate in prayer in a completely different—and much more valuable—manner?

So often we use prayer as a vehicle to get us to a desired destination. We need provision, so we pray. We need anointing, so we pray. We need healing or deliverance, or cleansing, so we pray. But what if prayer is not the vehicle that brings us *to* our destination? Rather, what if it *is the destination*?

Prayer is not simply a step of the journey; prayer *is the journey.* When we realize this, we will understand prayer as a continual conversation with God. And as I think back, I'm pretty sure this is a truth my grandfather fully grasped.

In Genesis, we read about the garden of Eden. Adam and Eve had committed a sin—they had eaten the forbidden fruit—and now their eyes were open. The imagery the Word of God painted here is that in the cool of the day, God comes walking through the garden, seeking to talk with them. Can you imagine what that would look like? In the garden of Eden, in the cool of the day, maybe in the afternoon, God comes walking along. Why is he taking a walk in the garden? He's looking for Adam and Eve so he can have a conversation with them.

As God walks, he asks, "Where are you?" God, who is omnipresent—everywhere at every time—and omniscient—all-knowing—asks Adam and Eve, "Where are you?" He knew where they were, obviously, but they were hiding. They were avoiding this conversation with their Creator. Their sin had led them to avoid God; their disobedience had brought separation. In our lives, sin also separates us from God. Nonetheless, the powerful question God asks them still remains for us to answer, "Where are you?"

Do you think God didn't know where Adam and Eve were? Do you think God didn't know the exact pinpoint location, without a GPS, where Adam and Eve were hiding? Have you ever stood in a room that was full or sat at a table with other people and felt completely ignored? Though the room was full, no one was paying attention to you. Have you ever attended an event one day and then the following day you ran into someone who said, "I saw you there," and you said, "I didn't see you there"? It is easy to ignore and be ignored.

So many times, God walks into our lives in the cool of the day, and even though he knows exactly where we are, he asks, "Where are you?" Maybe the question God was asking Adam and Eve was not for him. Maybe it was for them.

WHERE ARE YOU?
AN ENCOUNTER WITH JESUS

Consider this question: What was going on in the heart of God when he asked the question: "Where are you?" Was his intention to find Adam and then wipe him off the face of the planet? Did God ask the question because he planned to give Adam the silent treatment and never speak to him again? Or was God's heart and divine intention to ask the question that ultimately revealed his plan for redemption and restoration?

There were certainly consequences to Adam's disobedience, but the heart of God was filled with compassion and love. We know this because God's plan is revealed throughout Scripture where he is always reaching out to humanity.

Don't miss this: How we view God's heart toward us determines our pursuit of intimacy with him. Listen as he asks the same question of you: "Where are you?" And remember, his heart's intention isn't to harm you or never speak to you again. Who would want to pursue closeness with that kind of "god"?

Instead, imagine this kind of God. Imagine that you're a parent of a small child. You're in a busy shopping mall during the holidays. Hundreds of people are crowding the aisles, hustling to get to the next store, elbowing their way through the halls, and shoving to keep their place in line. Your preschooler is intrigued and distracted by everything in sight. And then it happens. You're focused on a conversation with the salesperson, you look around and your child is gone. You panic. You retrace your steps. Over and over, you're thinking to yourself, *Where are you?*

Consider the emotions flooding your heart. You may be irritated at your child's impulsiveness and scared about the dangers of being separated, but underneath all that is your heart of compassion. Your irritation is no match for the compassion you feel as you imagine your child alone and afraid. The question, "Where are you?" is motivated by love. Now imagine the relief you feel after being reunited with your child; the joy you would feel when the relationship and security are restored.

Though God never has and never will lose sight of us, perhaps we may fail to see him at times. Reflect again on your view of God, just in case you've seen God in another way. *This* is the real God. This is the God who is longing to love you and to intimately relate with you. This kind of God prompts our pursuit of him.

"Yet the LORD longs to be gracious to you; therefore he will rise up to show you compassion. For the LORD is a God of justice. Blessed are all who wait for him!" (Isaiah 30:18). Pause quietly to meditate on the Lord. Use your imagination to picture Jesus sitting at the Father's right hand. *You* have been the lost child, anxious and uncertain. And now he sees you with joy and excitement. He arises with compassion in his heart to embrace you. Allow your heart to celebrate this kind of Jesus!

L3. *Experiencing God as he really is through deepened intimacy with him.*

When prayer becomes more than an event, more than just a hammer in a tool bag that we grab when we need it; when prayer becomes a constant, ongoing conversation with God, we will begin to recognize the countless times we have ignored him. When prayer becomes conversation, God will ask us, "Where are you?" so we can answer, "I am right here."

I learned a lot about farming from Granddaddy. To feed livestock, a person needs hay, so my grandfather grew hay. We would cut, rake, bale, and store the hay so we could feed it to the cows. Hay can be gathered into large rolls that must be lifted and transported by a tractor, or it can be gathered into smaller bales (usually rectangle-shaped) that can be lifted by hand. Most of the time, our hay was gathered into the smaller bales, which meant we had to pick up every single bale by hand and throw it onto the trailer. We would then drive the trailer back to the barn where we'd unload all the bales to protect them from the weather until winter, when we'd feed it to the livestock.

As a boy, it seemed as if we only hauled hay on the hottest days of the year. It was hard work, and almost every child and grandchild participated, except for the youngest of the young. We recruited as many people as possible to help so the work would go faster. It was hard work, but it was a joy to participate together to accomplish something that meant so much to my grandfather.

I look back at those times with joy, but I also I remember what it felt like before I was old enough to help, when I was too little to be of much use. I wanted to contribute like everyone else, but I was just too small to lift a bale of hay. My father must have seen this longing inside of me as a little boy, because he would often call out to me, "Can you come help me pick up this bale of hay and put it on the trailer?" And all fifty pounds of me would run over to grab one end of that seventy-five-pound bale of hay, hoist it up, and throw it onto the trailer with all my might.

"I did it!" I would proclaim. "I put the hay on the trailer!" I'm sure my dad just laughed, knowing that he had done all the lifting and pulling—I was only there with my hands on the hay. But it felt so wonderful to believe I was a part of this family chore.

As I think back to moments like these, I realize God seems to work in a similar manner. God doesn't need you or me, but he loves us so much that he calls us over to participate in what he's doing: "I have a weight that is far too heavy for you, but if you'll come over, we'll pick it up together. We'll accomplish more together than you ever thought you could. It's my strength that gets the job done. It's your cooperation with me that makes it enjoyable for us both."

God doesn't need us, but he loves us so much that he calls us to participate in what he's doing.

Only in constant conversation with God can we come to these realizations. This is how the participation begins. To help with the bale, I had to hear Daddy's voice calling to me. I had to listen. I had to know his voice. We come to know the voice of God through constant conversation. In such conversation, we hear God calling us to participate with him in the work he's doing in this world. That's why Granddaddy prayed; that's why we pray. John 14:11–14 says:

> Believe me when I say that I am in the Father and the Father is in me; or at least believe on the evidence of the works themselves. Very truly I tell you, whosoever believes in me will do the works I have been doing, and they will do even greater works than these, because I am going to the Father. And I will do whatever you ask in my name, so that the Father may be glorified in the Son. You may ask me for anything in my name, and I will do it.

On January 8, 2015, my younger brother, Jason, passed away. I've told many that, between the two of us, I believe the Lord gave Jason all the good looks, charm, and charisma. He was the funniest person I ever met. He had suffered with addiction problems most of his adult life. He was a wonderful brother, but he struggled to be free from the strongholds of addiction. He had been in and out of many rehab programs. Our family tried to walk through Jason's struggles with him; I'm not sure I supported him enough or gave him what he needed, but I always wanted to help. Most of the time, I didn't know what to do or how to do it. We loved him greatly.

Before Jason died, however, the Lord began to speak to my heart about addiction and how we could and should respond to the needs of the addicted. There are addicts all over the world, probably some who will read this book. Addicts are not second-class people; they are not terrible people. If you have an addiction that you can't seem to shake, you're not a horrible person. You have a stronghold in your life. And like everyone who wrestles with sin or any sort of bondage, God desperately loves you, and he will not leave you to struggle alone. He will lead you to the right people, the right program, and the right help, if you'll ask him; if you start a conversation with him about your struggle.

One day, I told my brother I wanted to have a recovery program at Peerless Road Church, where I served as pastor. I asked his opinion on the different programs available. His response g  my attention: "All of those programs you mentioned are great.   if you think you can run any of them, you are wrong. You c 

lead a recovery program—because no one will listen to you. You've never done drugs. You've never experienced what they have experienced. You need a recovered addict to run the program. Those struggling with addiction will listen then." And, somehow, even though this was a new way of thinking for me, I understood.

I began to pray a strange prayer: "God, send us a drug addict." I knew we not only needed God to send us an addict, but we also needed to see that addict delivered from addiction through the power of Jesus. Then we would need that delivered addict to be willing to lead a program in our church so we could see other addicts delivered too. Put simply—we needed a miracle.

During this time, I had a conversation with one of my friends, Kenny Alderman. Kenny was a member of our church. He and his wife, Jamie, both worked in our church's SERVE ministry, which met the needs of our community through food assistance and other outreach programs. I knew Kenny's heart for the hurting, so I told him, "Kenny, I need you to help me pray about something. I need you to pray with me that God sends us a drug addict."

He looked at me, laughed, and said, "Pastor, it sounds like you pray the worst prayers I've ever heard!" We both laughed. He said, "Most people pray for fun things: money, family, good times, but you want me to pray for a drug addict? If you're sure that's what we need, we'll do it." We all need friends who are willing to pray with us, even when the request seems absurd.

I continued to ask the Lord to send a drug addict, even though I could not see in my mind exactly how it would all work out. I believe in deliverance—I cannot fathom a gospel that fails ͻ free us from our chains. Such a gospel would not be the gospel at all. That's not the power of Jesus Christ. That's not deliverance. I serve a God who not only forgives, but he sanctifies. He forgives and delivers. Our lives are different when we experience transformation through Jesus.

As I continued to pray for God to send us an addict, one day a man came into the church office. I received a message that there was someone there to see me. Like most pastors, I was pressed for time, but I agreed to see him. I ushered him into the conference room and he sat at one end of the long table while I took a seat at the other end.

He said, "My name is Russ Coffey. I have a drug and alcohol rehabilitation program called Anchor Point. We do not have anywhere in this city to meet. We've moved nine times. We cannot find a place to call home. Do you think your church would be interested in letting us come and participate in ministry with this church? Do you think Peerless Road Church could be the place we finally call 'home'?"

I was stunned. I sat in silence, overwhelmed for a moment. I'm not sure I was able to comprehend what God was doing or how God was answering the prayer we had been praying. I looked at him and said, "You don't know this, but God sent you to this place. You couldn't know it, but I've asked God to send one addict, just one person, who would be delivered and help us minister to those struggling with addiction. But God isn't sending just one; he's sending many. Yes, you can call this church 'home'!"

When we participate in what God is doing, he does so much more than we could ever imagine or even ask for. Maybe I could handle one addict; I could "manage" the life of one delivered addict. But there's no way I could pick up a hundred. But when

God is your Father, he says, "Come, work with me. I will pick up more than you could ever pick up without me."

And so, in a moment, when Russ Coffey said, "Our ministry wants to come and partner with Peerless Road Church," he offered us—instantly—a program that brings between seventy-five to a hundred and fifty people into the church gym every Tuesday night. And they're all seeking deliverance. God is a big God who is interested in us. He often answers our prayers in such a spectacular way that we could have never imagined.

The last time I saw my brother before he died, I reminded him of the words he had spoken to me about finding an addict to start a ministry. I said, "You know we have a ministry now at our church that is touching the lives of many addicts. And it's all because of you; because of what you told me. After you said those things, I began to pray and God began to answer."

Prayer is a conversation. It cannot be something we pull out of a tool bag when we desperately need to do a specific job. Prayer cannot become something we use to get what we want. Rather, it is an intimate, ongoing exchange with God. Prayer allows us to participate with God in his love and work for humanity.

When we hear a sermon or read a book about prayer, we often get inspired to pray more. We fix it in our minds: "This week, I'm going to pray more." It happens every time. But I'm not asking you to do that, because you'll probably fail—just like all the other times before that. You wanted to pray more, and you did well for a little while. But then life got in the way.

I'm asking you to transform the way you pray, to talk to God as he walks with you, when he calls out to you, "Where are you?" Don't use prayer as a tool, but as a genuine, engaging, give-and-take conversation with God throughout your day. Prayer is not the vehicle that takes us where we're going; it *is* where we're going.

NOT THE PATH BUT THE DESTINATION: A MOMENT OF FELLOWSHIP

Remember the childhood story of *Alice's Adventures in Wonderland*? When Alice found herself lost in the Enchanted Forest, she arrived at a crossroads. There were several paths she could choose through the forest. Alice was confused, uncertain, and insecure about which road to take. With bewilderment, Alice looked up in the tree above her and noticed the Cheshire Cat.

"Which way do I go?" Alice asked.

The cat posed a critical, relevant question: "Well, where are you going?"

"I really don't know," Alice replied.

The cat's response was insightful: "Then it really doesn't matter!"

As a follower of Jesus, it matters where we are going. Many Jesus-followers seem a lot like Alice. We're unsure of where we are headed. We're confused by the maze of events, programs, and projects offered along the Christian life. The apostle Paul shared his burden for the believers in Corinth facing similar complexities: "But I am afraid that ... your minds may somehow be led astray from your sincere and pure devotion to Christ" (2 Corinthians 11:3).

Where am I headed as a follower of Jesus? The simple answer is in our identity. Followers of Jesus are headed toward Jesus! *He* is the destination. His life and character are our goal. His purposes become our passions, and prayer without ceasing becomes our identity:

I no longer live, but Christ lives in me. (Galatians 2:20)

He must increase, but I must decrease. (John 3:30 NASB)

Pause with a partner or small group, and with yielded hearts, express your desire to *decrease* in your thoughts and attitudes, your decisions and perspectives ... in order that he might *increase*!

L10. *Practicing the presence of the Lord, yielding to the Spirit's work of Christlikeness.*

We need to pray for each other. Prayer is ministry. In fact, it is missionary work to pray. Paul said in Romans 8:26–27:

In the same way, the Spirit helps us in our weakness. We do not know what we ought to pray for, but the Spirit himself intercedes for us through wordless groans. And he who searches our hearts knows the mind of the Spirit, because the Spirit intercedes for God's people in accordance with the will of God.

What I'm talking about here is Spirit-empowered prayer. Spirit-empowered prayer is when you enter a time of prayer, a conversation with God, and pray for people who are bruised and hurting, but you don't know where they are bruised and hurting. But the Spirit knows because he "searches all things"; he knows the mind of God.

The Holy Spirit will take over and pray in ways that I cannot. The Spirit begins to pray, and we enter again into a conversation with God where we do the missionary work of prayer. We begin to pray for people with needs we don't understand, in situations we cannot know.

We all need to see that prayer as conversation with God is a powerful ministry everyone can participate in. People need us to enter into prayer for them. There are so many hurting, addicted, lonely, broken, and lost people in my life, and while I can't possibly know every one of their needs, God knows. I want to pray for them, and I want the Holy Spirit to intercede through my words to our heavenly Father on their behalf. Being Holy Spirit empowered allows us to lift more than we could ever lift alone. We are surrendering to the work of God in us. It should be the desire of every Christian to follow God wherever his Sprit leads us and participate in communion with God as he directs.

Prayer does not move mountains; it is God who moves mountains. Prayer is not the answer; God is the answer. Prayer is not the key; God is the key.

A long time ago, a respected leader in our movement, who was known to be a great man of prayer, encouraged us to be people who engaged in "prevailing prayer," prayer that perseveres until it breaks through. I want to model a life of prevailing prayer that enables me to break through every bondage, every stronghold, every insecurity, every loss, every sin, and every wrong. I want to model a life of prevailing prayer that enables me to live victoriously in Christ, no matter the circumstances.

> *Prevailing prayer occurs when I have carried on*
> *a conversation with God, until I can finally, and truly,*
> *give him all the cares of this world that trouble me.*

What is prevailing prayer? Is it prayer that always gets me what I want? No. Prevailing prayer occurs when I have carried on a conversation with God, until I can finally, and truly, give him all the cares of this world that trouble me. A prayer is answered once God holds it in his hands, once God has taken that thing and said, "This is mine now." I want to lay my needs before the Lord. I want to have a conversation with him about it, saying, "God, I can't bear this anymore. Will you take it?"

And God always says, "Yes, I will take it. Cast all your cares on me. I don't just care about you; I care *for* you. See, you don't even have to care how this turns out. I am doing the caring. Trust me."

I want to be a person of prayer because prayer is conversation with God. I want to pray because God invites me to participate with him in his love for all humanity and his mission of restoration. And I want to pray and be a person of prayer, because even when I don't know what to say, the Spirit knows and he can pray in me and through me.

Don't take this information and say, "I'm never missing another prayer meeting," or, "I'm going to pray more. I'm going to do this more. I'm going to come to this or that more." Instead of those pronouncements, would you instead now consider prayer a conversation with God?

What if he is asking you as you read this, "Where are you?" Why would he ask that? He knows where you are. He's asking you because you need to know where you are. And you need to know where he is. You can find him, and yourself, when you finally learn to talk to God in prayer.

EMPOWERED BY THE SPIRIT: AN EXPERIENCE OF SCRIPTURE

But as for me, my prayer is to You, O Lord, at an acceptable time;
O God, in the greatness of Your lovingkindness,
Answer me with Your saving truth. (Psalm 69:13 NASB)

To You I lift up my eyes,
O You who are enthroned in the heavens! (Psalm 123:1 NASB)

Be filled with the Spirit. (Ephesians 5:18 NASB)

A life that's lived in the Spirit enjoys and is empowered by intimacy with God. Our self-interests distract us from pursuing Jesus and living lives of communion with him. Spend the next few moments experiencing Psalm 69 and 123. Let your prayer be to God. Ask him to answer by allowing you to experience his fullness. Lift your eyes to heaven and call upon the Lord.

Imagine that God now asks you the question he asked of Adam and Eve, "Where are you?". Be reassured that his heart is filled with compassion, and he longs to relate to you.

Pause in prayer. Yield to the fullness of his Spirit. Say yes to him and his invitation of communion. In response to his pursuit and probing question, "Where are you?" pray these words:

Here I am, Lord. Send me into a journey of intimate conversation and daily communication with you. I want to hear your saving truth. Speak it to me. I lift my eyes to heaven and I call upon you to _____.

 L9. *Faithful stewardship and exercise of the gifts of the Spirit for empowered living and service.*

Chapter 2

How to Approach God in Prayer

There is a powerful verse found in Luke 11:1: "One day Jesus was praying in a certain place. When he finished, one of his disciples said to him, 'Lord, teach us to pray, just as John taught his disciples.'" When we read the Gospels, we see that Jesus was not just someone who prayed sporadically; rather, he prayed constantly. He prayed so much that his disciples asked him to teach them how to pray.

The request they made—"Lord, teach us to pray"—was important. They wanted to interact with the Father in the same way they heard and saw Jesus continually interacting with the Father. We've probably all witnessed someone doing something we've never done before. When we ask them, "Would you show me how to do that?" we aren't really asking them to do it again; we're asking them to show *us* how to do it. The disciples didn't merely want to see Jesus pray more; they wanted to learn to pray for themselves.

When we hear a message on prayer, several things may come to mind. Our first thought is generally, *I don't pray enough. Surely the answer is to pray more.* Some of you may have already had that run through your head as you've been reading this book. But when the disciples asked Jesus to teach them to pray, I don't believe they were talking strictly about quantity. It wasn't about simply praying more often. They wanted to experience prayer as Jesus experienced it. They wanted to improve the *quality* of their prayers, not just the *quantity* of their prayers.

God opens himself up to us through our redemption, and by his grace he shows us who he is. Prayer is the way for us, in turn, to open ourselves up to God. He has offered himself to us through Jesus Christ, but now, through the gift of prayer, we offer ourselves back to him.

The disciples were not seeking a recipe for prayer. So many times, in messages, books, or lessons on prayer, we are looking for a recipe we can follow in order to have our prayers answered or to make prayer seem easier. We're looking for a key that will unlock our prayer lives: "Give me the key! Give me the prayer of faith to get God to do exactly what I want him to do. How can I get my prayers answered?"

We think there must be magic when it comes to prayer. If I put the key into the lock and turn it just the right way, God will do exactly what I want him to do. But the disciples weren't looking for a magical key. They were not asking to be taught how to pray so they could cast out devils. They were not asking to be taught how to pray so they could open blind eyes. They were not even asking to be taught how to pray so they could feed five thousand people.

No! They wanted to learn how to converse with the Creator of the universe.

When Jesus teaches them on prayer, he says:

> And when you pray, do not be like the hypocrites, for they love to pray standing in the synagogues and on the street corners to be seen by others. Truly I tell you, they have received their reward in full. But when you pray, go into your room, close the door and pray to your Father, who is unseen. Then your Father, who sees what is done in secret, will reward you. And when you pray, do not keep on babbling like pagans, for they think they will be heard because of their many words. Do not be like them, for your Father knows what you need before you ask him.
>
> This, then, is how you should pray: "Our Father in heaven, hallowed be your name, your kingdom come, your will be done, on earth as it is in heaven. Give us today our daily bread. And forgive us our debts, as we also have forgiven our debtors. And lead us not into temptation, but deliver us from the evil one."
>
> For if you forgive other people when they sin against you, your heavenly Father will also forgive you. (Matthew 6:5–14)

What is prayer? It is communion with God; it is conversation with the Father. The conditions in which I pray, as well as my attitude and thoughts as I pray, are important. But Jesus opens the essentials of prayer to his disciples here, allowing them to see what he did when he entered a conversation with the Father.

> *Jesus opens the essentials of prayer to his disciples,*
> *allowing them to see what he did when he entered a*
> *conversation with the Father.*

Is it possible for you to think about prayer differently? I want you to think, "How can I communicate with God?" I don't want you to feel guilty about possibly not praying enough, nor do I want you to feel proud if you think you do pray enough. I'm sure 90 percent of us would say, "I don't pray enough. So surely I must stir myself up and figure out how to have enough time to pray more or God won't bless me." Feeling that way accomplishes nothing and can become counterproductive to our prayer life. I am praying that the Holy Spirit would capture the heart of each of us, and that he would say to you and to me, "I want you to learn how to interact with me more deeply."

People interact in different ways. You and I are different people; we have different personalities. Not only that, but all the people around us have different personalities as well. Some are talkers, while some barely say a word. Jesus recognized that we are all different—in fact, he made us that way. The type of personality we have should not be an inhibitor to our conversation with God.

When Jesus began instructing us how to pray, he did something that was critical for us to understand if we desire to communicate with God as he did. He opened with, "Our Father in heaven, hallowed be your name" (Matthew 6:9). If we want to pray as Jesus did, we must see God as Jesus saw him—as our loving heavenly Father.

LEARNING TO PRAY:
AN ENCOUNTER WITH JESUS

"Lord, teach us to pray" (Luke 11:1). The disciples who lived and walked and were closest to Jesus apparently needed help with prayer. It's no wonder that you and I need the same. So where might we begin a lesson on prayer? Perhaps we could benefit from seeing the face of Jesus, which will help us see the Father.

Set aside the next few moments to be still before the Lord. Focus your mind and heart on Jesus. Let this be a moment of personal communication between you and the Savior. Now imagine the face of Jesus as he sits beside you. With a tender voice and an outstretched hand, he makes a personal invitation just to you: "Come to me. I want to relate to you in prayer (see Matthew 11:28). I am available to you. I am accessible. I am within your reach. I long for closeness and communication with you. Pure and simple: I love you."

Honor Jesus with the response of your heart. Talk to him with words like these:

Jesus, when I imagine hearing these words and how you long for me to join you in prayer, my heart is moved with _____ because _____.

And as a final step in learning to pray, imagine that you now join Jesus in praying to the Father. Picture yourself kneeling beside the Savior, and together you express your gratitude for the privilege of prayer. Jesus reminds us that he and the Father are one; he is the perfect expression of our heavenly Father (see John 17:21). If you can talk to

Jesus, you can pray to God. Honor the Father with these words of reverence:

Heavenly Father, I am grateful to be able to talk to you. When I imagine being able to communicate to the almighty God, I feel _____ because _____.

L10. *Practicing the presence of the Lord, yielding to the Spirit's work of Christlikeness.*

How do you feel about communicating with God? More importantly, how *are* you communicating with God? The psalmist said it this way: "As the deer pants for streams of water, so my soul pants for you, my God" (Psalm 42:1).

How we approach God is important. Some people scream, acting as if God is unable to hear them unless they shout. Other people pray very, very quietly. Some people pray for a long time, and some people pray short prayers. I want us to ask ourselves, "When I pray, am I only using words, or am I actually communicating with God? And is God able to communicate with me? Do I listen as much as I speak?" If prayer is a conversation, listening is just as important, if not more important, than speaking.

In Luke 18:9–14, Jesus tells a parable about the importance our attitude when we communicate with God:

To some who were confident of their own righteousness and looked down on everyone else, Jesus told this parable: "Two men went up to the temple to pray, one a Pharisee and the other a tax collector. The Pharisee stood by himself and prayed: 'God, I thank you that I am not like other people—robbers, evildoers, adulterers—or even like this tax collector. I fast twice a week and give a tenth of all I get.'

"But the tax collector stood at a distance. He would not even look up to heaven, but beat his breast and said, 'God, have mercy on me, a sinner.'

"I tell you that this man, rather than the other, went home justified before God. For all those who exalt themselves will be humbled and those who humble themselves will be exalted."

We must approach God with an attitude of sincerity: "God, I have not come to manipulate you. I have not come to ask you to do something for me." Prayer is not merely asking God for all we need or want. It is interaction with the Creator of the universe. Prayer is an essential way in which God transforms us into his likeness and image. Our hearts must be broken when we approach the living God. Without humility and brokenness, we will be like the Pharisee who prayed, "God, I thank you that I am not like other people" (Luke 18:11).

Prayer is not merely asking God for all we need or want.
It is interaction with the Creator of the universe.

If we approach God without humility, feeling as if we deserve something or that God owes us, we will surely struggle to communicate with him. But when we come to him humbly, saying, "Lord, I come to interact with you as my Father. I come to interact with you as the Creator of the universe; as one who loves me. Lord, I want to have relationship with you," God's heart will be open to us. With this heart posture, we can encounter God anew through prayer.

When we approach our heavenly Father, there must remain a certain "awe" in our communication with him. Our conversation with God is always sacred because God is sacred. Therefore, we approach God, remembering that it is by his grace and mercy that he has allowed us to interact with him, and it is through him we live, move, and have our being.

Next, Jesus begins teaching his disciples to pray by praising the Father. He starts out by saying, "This then is how you should pray: 'Our Father in heaven, hallowed be your name.'"

First, we praise God for who he is. We praise him because he is our Father. What did it mean for Jesus to pray to his Father? He always approached God as Father. We should never approach God as Santa Claus or as if he is far away. We should approach God as our loving Father who is worthy of praise, not because of what he has done, but simply because of who he is—the Creator of the universe.

We find Jesus praying yet again just before going to the cross:

After Jesus said this, he looked toward heaven and prayed: "Father, the hour has come. Glorify your Son, that your Son may glorify you. For you granted him authority over all people that he might give eternal life to all those you have given him. Now this is eternal life: that they know you, the only true God, and Jesus Christ, whom you have sent. I have brought you glory on earth by finishing the work you gave me to do. And now, Father, glorify me in your presence with the glory I had with you before the world began." (John 17:1–5)

When we truly see God as Father, we realize that not only is God the Father responsible for us, but we are responsible to him too. Jesus begins his directions concerning prayer by instructing us to say, "Our Father."

I am convinced, as a man in my forties and after a lifetime of serving God, that our relationship with our earthly fathers has an impact on our relationship with our heavenly Father. In his mercy, God blessed me with an earthly father who loved me and always showed me his love. As I was growing up, every day my brother and I would get a hug and a kiss from our dad (and from our mother too), and we always heard, "I love you."

My father and mother loved me, hugged me, and embraced me constantly. Even in my high school years, I remember hugs and kisses from Mom and Dad at bedtime, which always ended with, "I love you." I was accepted and loved by my father, and his love for me has undoubtedly formed my view of God as my Father. My dad made it extremely easy for me to see God as the loving, accepting, and caring heavenly Father that he is.

When I think about my heavenly Father, I think of someone who reaches down to love me and who continually tells me he loves me. But there are some of you reading this who have had a different experience with your father. Learning to interact with the heavenly Father as you interact with your earthly father may be difficult for you because you are still in pain from the hurts caused by your earthly father. When Jesus said to pray, "Our Father who is in heaven," he was saying to you, "If you do not know how to or are unable to interact with your father, I want to show you what the real Father is like—he is a Father who will love you, a Father who will say that he loves you, someone who will embrace you with the love of a Father."

I am praying there will be healing in your heart, and that you will experience the wholeness that only Jesus Christ can give. Later on, we will look at what Jesus says about forgiveness—how we can be forgiven and how he will enable us to forgive others. If you didn't feel or don't feel the love and affection of an earthly father for whatever reason, I'm praying that you will feel the loving presence of the heavenly Father. It is my hope that you will experience the acceptance of God you've never experienced. Do not believe the lie of satan that your heavenly Father doesn't love you. He does love you, just as you are. And you will never have to earn his love.

God desires for us to interact with him because he is our loving heavenly Father who desires to communicate with us. He wants to know you. This understanding, when brought into our prayer life, can enable us to experience God's overwhelming love for us, his children. Romans 8:14–15 reminds us:

> For those who are led by the Spirit of God are the children of God. The Sprit you received does not make you slaves, so that you live in fear again; rather, the Spirit you received brought about your adoption to sonship. And by him we cry, "*Abba*, Father."

HIS GREAT PLEASURE:
AN ENCOUNTER WITH JESUS

God decided in advance to adopt us into his own family by bringing us to himself through Jesus Christ. This is what he wanted to do, and it gave him great pleasure. (Ephesians 1:5 NLT)

Pause for a few moments and slowly read the scripture verse above. Make it personal: "God decided in advance to adopt *me* into his own family ... and it gave him great pleasure." Now imagine Jesus sitting beside you. He puts his arm around you and smiles with great pride as he explains, "Just think—the Father has chosen you to be a part of our family. As your heavenly Father, he wanted to provide for you, protect you, care for you, and guide you, so he sent me to bring you to himself. It gives him great pleasure to see *you* as part of his family."

Allow the Holy Spirit to reaffirm the truth of this relationship and confirm your adoption into the family of God. Now express your thanks for God's amazing gift:

Father, I am grateful you decided to adopt me into your family because _____.

I am amazed at what you went through to have me join your family, and I thank you for _____.

L4. *Rejoicing regularly in my identity as his beloved.*

His adoption, his pulling in, this closeness that we now have with God, is not something we can do without. It is something we need: "Lord, help us to interact by the Holy Spirit!"

We are learning how to step into a relationship with God. We are stepping into an opportunity to interact with God the Father. You are opening your heart up to him as he is opening himself up to you. Listen to what the psalmist said directly to God in Psalm 19:1–11:

> The heavens declare the glory of God;
>> the skies proclaim the work of his hands.
> Day after day they pour forth speech;
>> night after night they reveal knowledge.
> They have no speech, they use no words;
>> no sound is heard from them.
> Yet their voice goes out into all the earth,
>> their words to the ends of the world.
> In the heavens God has pitched a tent for the sun.
>> It is like a bridegroom coming out of his chamber,
>> like a champion rejoicing to run his course.
> It rises at one end of the heavens
>> and makes its circuit to the other;
>> nothing is deprived of its warmth.
> The law of the LORD is perfect,
>> refreshing the soul.
> The statutes of the LORD are trustworthy,
>> making wise the simple.
> The precepts of the LORD are right,
>> giving joy to the heart.

The commands of the LORD are radiant,
> giving light to the eyes.
The fear of the LORD is pure,
> enduring forever.
The decrees of the LORD are firm,
> and all of them are righteous.
They are more precious than gold,
> than much pure gold;
they are sweeter than honey,
> than honey from the honeycomb.
By them is your servant warned;
> in keeping them there is great reward.

I will praise him for who he is: "God, I praise you because you are merciful and good and loving and kind and warm. You reach out to us in our brokenness, even in our pain, even when we are weak, even when we know nothing. You approach us in grace and love. Lord, I praise you for all your attributes, your greatness, and your power. You are tremendous. You are the Creator. You are all things! Who am I that you are mindful of me? I praise you because you are God. Your personality is so wonderful!"

I approach God and praise him because of his attributes. I also approach him and praise him because of what he has done for me. As we desire to enter into a time of tremendous prayer and interaction with God, as we hallow his name, we should learn to praise God for what he has done for us individually.

Recalling the blessings of God can fuel such a time of praise.

You remember when you did not have enough money and God made a way; you remember when you were in desperate need of healing and God made the way; you remember all those things God did for you. Simply recounting all the blessings of God and answered prayers can dramatically transform your prayer life.

As I begin to recall God's work in my life and in my family's life, my mind immediately goes to a dreadful day in 2010. On this day, my family received the news that no family wants to hear. My wife, Renee, was diagnosed with cancer.

I'm sure this disease in some way has affected most of us, either directly or indirectly, perhaps in our own family or in the family of a friend. "Cancer" is a scary word. It immediately grips us with fear. We went through those dark days of treatment and surgeries together. They were scary days, but now Renee is cancer free! And we praise God for this. For us, this is a powerful image of praise when we consider how God never left us alone, even in her most difficult times of treatment.

When I am reminded of the emotional and spiritual battles we endured through this time, I praise and adore God most of all for how close he was to us. I praise him because his will was to allow our family to see her healed and restored.

A YIELDED HEART:
AN EXPERIENCE OF SCRIPTURE

What sorrow awaits those who argue with their Creator. (Isaiah 45:9 NLT)

Consider some of the recent challenges or difficult circumstances that God has sent your way. Are you making the choice to grow from them, or are you quarreling or arguing with God about them? The prophet Isaiah reminds us that quarreling with our Creator will only bring us sorrow. But if quarreling with the Creator only brings sorrow, then how should we respond?

We gain insight into the answer by looking at how Jesus responded to the Father in the midst of his pain and suffering. Jesus' response was to *yield*. His commitment to yield was so strong that he described it as his very nourishment: "'My food,' said Jesus, 'is to do the will of him who sent me and to finish his work'" (John 4:34).

One of the ways we can express our love to the Father is to yield to the Holy Spirit and yield to his ways for our life. We express love to the Father when we yield ourselves to the Creator of all things—even before we know his plan. In other words, one of the simplest ways to love God is to say, "Yes, Lord, now what would you have me do?"

Spend some time expressing your yielded heart to the Lord. Declare that the quarreling is over:

Lord, I acknowledge your work in my life, and I yield to the Holy Spirit's fullness and strength. Continue your Spirit's work in me so that I will never again quarrel with you over what is best for my life. I trust what you are doing is according to your perfect plan for me. Help me to trust you when I doubt, Lord. Help me to trust you in the midst of pain and uncertainty. I yield to you specifically in these ways _____.

L9. *Faithful stewardship and exercise of the gifts of the Spirit for empowered living and service.*

It's easy to praise God now that Renee has been healed; it's easy to praise God once the cancer is gone. However, I know how hard it can be to praise God during the struggle. As I've learned through many difficult moments, I always have a reason to praise God. I can always recall a blessing that will push me into a moment of praise. Whatever you may be walking through today, you have something to praise God for. You can find a way to praise God in your valleys.

In these dark valleys, it is often difficult to pray at all. This is one of the reasons I am convinced God wants us to be a part of a local community of believers (church) so that others can help us pray when we cannot. But if you can't pray, then try praise: "Lord, I thank you that just a little while ago I was there, but now I'm here. God, I was broken but now I'm restored; I thank you for that."

A simple expression of gratitude opens to us a line of interaction with God. And so I praise him for what he's done for me. And you can praise him for what he's done for you. And if, for some reason, you simply cannot find a way to praise, then just tell God that very fact. Even speaking about your frustrations to God is still prayer.

Finally, another concept to consider in hallowing the name of God as we pray is to praise him for what he's done for *us,* corporately, as the people of God. Titus 3:3–8 says:

> At one time we too were foolish, disobedient, deceived and enslaved by all kinds of passions and pleasures. We lived in malice and envy, being hated and hating

one another. But when the kindness and love of God our Savior appeared, he saved us, not because of righteous things we had done, but because of his mercy. He saved us through the washing of rebirth and renewal by the Holy Spirit, whom he poured out on us generously through Jesus Christ our Savior, so that, having been justified by his grace, we might become heirs having the hope of eternal life. This is a trustworthy saying. And I want you to stress these things, so that those who have trusted in God may be careful to devote themselves to doing what is good. These things are excellent and profitable for everyone.

Don't just rejoice when God does something for you individually, but praise him for what he has done for others as well! Enter a time of praise for God's provision for your church family, your friends, and your community.

Often, the current Christian culture reduces Christianity to an individualist enterprise. However, serving Christ is not just an individual work. Christ uses others to mold us into his image and likeness. We need one another to fulfill God's will, and we need one another to grow. When I praise God for what he has done and is doing for others and not just for me, I am acknowledging that I am a part of God's mission in the world.

---

*Christ uses others to mold us into his image and likeness.
We need one another to fulfill God's will,
and we need one another to grow.*

◇

Pray today. Praise today. Speak with God today. If you feel your prayer life is challenged because you are struggling to see God as your Father, I want you to allow God to transform you and restore you as you accept him as your loving Father. Worship and interact with him as your Father, without impediment. I want us to praise God for the things he's done for us as individuals. And lastly, I want us to praise him for what he has done for all of us. Salvation! Justification! Renewal by the Spirit! Heirs of eternal life! Isaiah 53 says God has provided healing for us. We praise him for these things!

Don't let anyone tell you that prayer is not work. Anyone who says such a thing has obviously never done the work of prayer. Prayer is discipline, and it takes discipline. The discipline of prayer is difficult, but when taken up wholeheartedly, it is eternally rewarding.

Prayer is speaking to God and God speaking with us. Those quiet moments of prayer that Jesus spoke of in Matthew 6—entering the closet, the secret place—those moments are where much is accomplished. In these moments, I learn to praise God for who he is, thank him for what he has done for me, and thank him for what he has done for all of us.

THANKS FOR HIS FRIENDSHIP:
A MOMENT OF FELLOWSHIP

"I no longer call you servants, because a servant does not know his master's business. Instead, I have called you friends, for everything that I learned from my Father I have made known to you." (John 15:15)

Jesus desires a deep friendship with you. He desires to share with you, as his disciple, what he has learned from the Father. You have chosen to follow him, and he has chosen to share with you, reveal himself to you, and then communicate the gospel through you.

Pause for a moment to consider this wonderful privilege. The God of the universe wants to reveal himself to *you*. Because you are his disciple and his friend, Jesus wants to be vulnerable with you. How do you feel as you embrace the truth that Christ wants you to know the things that are on his heart? Respond to the Lord as his friend.

Make time to pray together with a mentor or small group. Share some moments of worship and praise for this kind of Jesus.

Lord Jesus, as I embrace the wonder of friendship with you, my heart responds with _____. When I consider that you want to share your heart with me and be vulnerable with me, I am moved with feelings of _____. Jesus, because I am so grateful that you want this kind of friendship with me, I am motivated to _____ (For example, spend more time reading the Bible; listen as well as talk to you in prayer; regularly ask you to reveal yourself in me.).

SPIRIT-EMPOWERED Faith

L7. Entering often into Spirit-led praise and worship.

Chapter 3

A Life of Prayer
Is a Life of Trust

If you've been reading this book over several days or weeks, how has your prayer life evolved in that course of time? Have you sensed a greater desire to draw closer to God through prayer?

In our last chapter, we read from Luke 11:1, where the disciples asked Jesus to teach them how to pray like John taught his disciples how to pray. Then we moved on to Matthew 6, looking at what Jesus said, thus expanding on their request:

> And when you pray, do not be like the hypocrites, for they love to pray standing in the synagogues and on the street corners to be seen by others. Truly I tell you, they have received their reward in full. But when you pray, go into your room, close the door and pray to your Father, who is unseen. Then your Father, who sees what is done in secret, will reward you. And when you pray, do not keep on babbling like pagans, for they think they will be heard because of their many words. Do not be like

them, for your Father knows what you need before you ask him.

This then is how you should pray: "Our Father in heaven, hallowed be your name, your kingdom come, your will be done, on earth as it is in heaven. Give us today our daily bread. And forgive us our debts, as we also have forgiven our debtors. And lead us not into temptation, but deliver us from the evil one."

For if you forgive other people when they sin against you, your heavenly Father will also forgive you. But if you do not forgive others their sins, your Father will not forgive your sins. (Matthew 6:5–15)

The disciples asked to have the type of communion with God that Jesus enjoyed. How can we enter a conversation with God that goes beyond a simple prayer event or a prayer vigil? How can we enter a place of rest with the Father that brings us into perpetual communion with him?

When we read the words of Jesus as he expounds on how to pray, we might assume he's talking about a manner of praying or a system of prayer. We may imagine that Jesus was about to reveal a formula for all our prayers to be assuredly answered: "Do this in prayer, and God will do this. Say this in prayer, and God will do that." But this is not what Jesus shared. In fact, the manner of prayer that Jesus taught was not a simple formula, but a lifestyle of communion—a way of daily, hourly, and even minute-by-minute communing with God our Father.

"Approach him as your Father," Jesus said. To us, that's just another way we see God. We call him Lord; we call him King of kings; we call him Jehovah. We call him the Great I Am. But Jesus said, "Call him Father." The more we call him "Father," the more we come to understand that prayer is the way in which we develop a familial, intimate relationship with God.

The parameters of the Father's kingdom are drawn so that the unlovable are loved, the unforgivable are forgiven, and the last are first—and I enter the work of this kingdom through prayer. Here, in prayer, I surrender my will, my rights, and my ambitions. I yield myself totally to the Father and join in his kingdom work.

> *In prayer, we surrender our will, rights, and ambitions.*
> *We yield ourselves totally to the Father and join*
> *in his kingdom work.*

Then Jesus teaches that communion with the Father is about much more than what is said. The request, "Give us this day our daily bread," speaks of more than just words. It is a lifestyle of trust we enter with our heavenly Father. We trust him to provide for us. How futile it would be as his children to take on the responsibility of securing for ourselves our daily provision. We ask him to give us our daily bread, our daily sustenance.

Throughout my childhood, I never took a thought of my own provision or of finding my daily food. My only concern was to be the best pretend cowboy I could possibly be; to learn how to ride my stick horse with great authority; to learn how to holster my toy pistol and draw it out of my plastic holster as quickly as possible. It was my job to take my small, green toy army men and line them up in perfect rows, battle after battle, with firecrackers firmly attached to their legs, ready to be lit at a moment's notice. That was my job.

But it was the job of my father to put food on our family's table. I took no thought whether there would be supper each night. When Mother called me to the table, I simply went, trusting that food would be there. I completely trusted that I would be fed. I never thought about it, which allowed me to be the best cowboy hero I could be.

The principle Jesus speaks to us as he says, "Our Father in heaven … Give us today our daily bread," is a principle we must believe and live out each day. If I, as a child, would have doubted my father's ability to provide for me and our family, it would have offended him. Likewise, if we doubt God's ability to provide for us, we offend him. So we trust him to supply every need.

This is not a lifestyle of laziness on our part; it is not that we don't care. It is not a lifestyle that says, "I won't do my part." Rather, it is a lifestyle that says, "God, I trust you to do your part. I trust that you will provide." In this manner, I honestly pray, "Give us today our daily bread."

As we say those words, we are learning to trust God. We are learning dependence and submission. We are learning to trust his perfect will for us. The will of God is bound together with the kingdom of God. We cannot say, "God, let your will be done in my life," without saying, "Let your kingdom come in my life."

FIX YOUR THOUGHTS:
AN ENCOUNTER WITH JESUS

Therefore, holy brothers and sisters, who share in the heavenly calling, fix your thoughts on Jesus. (Hebrews 3:1)

To fix our thoughts and hearts on Jesus is to relate intimately and lovingly to him. It means focusing our spiritual eyes and the emotions of our heart on the person of Jesus, not just his position. Fixing our thoughts on Jesus will look like yielding and submitting to him; it will mean moving beyond our rational beliefs about the historical Jesus. Fixing our thoughts on Jesus means seeing him and all that he is as a contemporary and present Savior. He can be trusted!

Fix your eyes on Jesus today. Imagine the Savior sitting on the throne of heaven at the right hand of God. He is the King of kings, and the earth is his footstool. Psalm 104:1 tells us that he is robed with honor and majesty. Let the eyes of your heart see the beautiful throne room, his majestic robes, and his royal stature. You see Christ's position, and your thoughts align with the beliefs about the Savior, but that's not the same as fixing your thoughts on the *person of Jesus*.

Pause now and fix the eyes of your heart on the character and person of Jesus. Imagine Christ saying these words just to you: "I am the one who sits on heaven's throne, but I love to call you my friend (see John 15:15). My name is Most High, the King of all the earth, but you can come to me anytime you desire. I am ready to listen to what you have to say. In fact, I lean in to hear your prayers (see Psalm 47:2; 17:6)."

Take the next few moments to thank the Father for being your ultimate provider. Share your gratitude for how he has met your needs according to his riches in glory (see Philippians 4:19). Yield yourself to a life of bold and believing prayer. Trust him with your present and future.

Heavenly Father, thank you for being my ultimate provider of _____. I'm grateful for how you have met my needs by _____. Because you are faithful, I trust you today to _____. I trust you to do your part. Because you are faithful, I trust you for _____ in the future.

 L9. *Faithful stewardship and exercise of the gifts of the Spirit for empowered living and service.*

When my daughter, Tayler, was young—probably around two years old—she loved to play a jumping game with me. She would run around our house, singing, playing, and jumping on everything she could reach. I loved playing with her. She loved it when I would place her on top of the dresser in our bedroom. It was about four feet tall, and since she was about two feet tall, for her it was like standing on top of a mountain. She loved to stand on top of that "mountain" and jump off into my arms. "Let's jump again!" she would say over and over again.

Each time, I would back up further and further, and she would jump into my arms, every time laughing and screaming, "Again, again!" She never, ever thought there was any chance that her father would not catch her. She knew from experience, but mostly from the love she felt from her father, that she could trust me and that there was no way I would allow her to fall. Trusting God can be a lot like this. I can trust him because I know that he will never let me fall.

Asking God to teach me to pray is not so I can have my way more often. I'm saying, "Lord, show me how to commune with you." When we pray for God to supply our daily bread, there are some important principles of trust we need to consider.

When we pray in this manner, we are first saying, "I will trust that God knows and cares for my needs." In Matthew 6:19, Jesus says in the Sermon on the Mount, "Do not store up for yourselves treasures on earth." It is sometimes difficult to read these words in the Bible; they're so easy to ignore. We may all be guilty of saying, "That's for you," or, "That's for them. It doesn't apply to my situation." But what he says here does apply to our situation. Jesus' words apply to all of us always.

What if that was the only verse of the Bible we ever received? What if we lived in a foreign land with no Scripture? What if we didn't have the whole cannon of Scripture, and somehow that was the only verse we could ever get? We read:

> "Do not store up for yourselves treasures on the earth, where moth and vermin destroy, and where thieves break in and steal. But store up for yourselves treasures in heaven, where moth and vermin do not destroy, and where thieves do not break in and steal." (Matthew 6:19–20)

How different would your life be if that was the only verse of Scripture you had?

Why would Jesus say those words in verses 19 and 20 that are so hurtful to my capitalistic ways, my greed, and my thirst for more? Jesus was not only putting a negative slant on greed, but he was also putting a positive slant on trust. We need not lay up for ourselves treasures on earth because God will take care of all our needs, if we trust him!

Jesus continues in Matthew 6:21, "For where your treasure is, there your heart will be also." The request, "Give us this day our daily bread," is linked to "your kingdom come, your will be done." We'll see that more clearly as we continue to unpack this prayer.

In verse 24, Jesus continues, "No one can serve two masters. Either you will hate the one and love the other or you will be devoted to the one and despise the other. You cannot serve God and money." Do you trust God? Do you serve a God who knows and cares about your needs? Then, Jesus said:

> Therefore I tell you, do not worry about your life, what you will eat or drink; or about your body, what you will wear. Is life not more than food, and the body more than clothes? Look at the birds of the air; they do not sow or reap or store away in barns, and yet your heavenly Father feeds them. Are you not much more valuable than they? Can any one of you by worrying add a single hour to your life?
>
> And why do you worry about clothes? See how the flowers of the field grow. They do not labor or spin. Yet I tell

you that not even Solomon in all his splendor was dressed like one of these. If that is how God clothes the grass of the field, which is here today and tomorrow is thrown into the fire, will he not much more clothe you—you of little faith? So do not worry, saying, "What shall we eat?" or, "What shall we drink?" or, "What shall we wear?" For the pagans run after all these things, and your heavenly Father knows that you need them. But seek first his kingdom and his righteousness, and all these things will be given to you as well. Therefore do not worry about tomorrow, for tomorrow will worry about itself. Each day has enough trouble of its own. (Matthew 6:25–34)

Jesus is throwing down the gauntlet for the church of today. Don't run after what unbelievers run after. He is calling his people to complete trust in him as their provider. When the systems and kingdoms of this present world call for fear and greed because they suggest we can never have enough, Christ is calling the church to be different because we can trust that he will supply our needs in Christ Jesus.

EXAMINE MY HEART:
AN EXPERIENCE OF SCRIPTURE

"... apart from me you can do nothing." (John 15:5)

Reflect again on the too-often-held belief that, "We can do this by ourselves." Pause quietly and ask the Father to reveal any tendency of this belief in you:

Heavenly Father, examine my heart. Do I tend to believe that I can do this life without you? What evidences of fear or greed are in me? What do you want me to see, hear, or experience instead? How can I please you by trusting you more?

Listen quietly for the Father's response.

Now imagine the following words from Jesus. Imagine that the Savior is speaking directly to you. Meditate on his words: "Remember, dear one—without me, you can do nothing."

Ask Jesus to change, strengthen, and empower you. Celebrate as you hear Jesus whisper these words to your spirit: "Don't forget: with God, all things are possible" (see Matthew 19:26). Receive the joy of this promise. Let it catalyze your hope and faith that he can be trusted. Bring him pleasure as you yield to his Spirit's work of purifying your heart. Wait to sense his presence and power in all your life.

SPIRIT-EMPOWERED *Faith*

L5. *Living with a passionate longing for purity and to please him in all things.*

Please understand, I believe everyone should work hard, everyone has a right to earn a living, and everyone has the right to prosper. We want to see our economy thrive; we want everything to go well in our lives. It is my desire that everyone has a job; I want everyone to have enough—plenty even. But Jesus says it clearly: The church cannot look like the corporate world. We are not a business. We are the church of the living God. All we possess is a gift from God. And when God is our source, there will always be enough.

> *We are the church of the living God.*
> *All we possess is a gift from God. And when God*
> *is our source, there will always be enough.*

Don't run after what those who trust in themselves run after. They're worried about budgets and offerings and dollars and materials. It's important to pay your bills—God expects you to do that—but don't be consumed with worry and fear over them. You see, "Give us today our daily bread," is inextricably wrapped up together with "Lord, let your kingdom come, your will be done."

My provision comes from God; it does not come from my job. Do I trust my job or do I trust my God for my paycheck? Trust is the glue that holds a vibrant prayer life together. When you say, "Give me this day my daily bread," you are entering into an agreement with God that says, "God, you are my Father, and as my Father I trust you to supply all my needs according to your riches in glory" (see Philippians 4:19).

I cannot fully surrender to the work of God's kingdom or to the working of his will in my life if I do not trust his provision. If I trust God, if I trust his plan for my life, if I can cooperate with him, then I am able to trust his provision.

Some of you have remarkable stories of God's provision. You've seen God's hand at work in moments of great need. I've heard of people who were down to their last loaf of bread when God miraculously provided groceries. Others have had bills to pay and no money in the bank, but God miraculously provided for their needs. Maybe you have a similar story to tell of God's provision.

At times, God wants to provide, while at other times, he gives us the opportunity to be the providers. Consider Luke 6:27–29:

> "But to you who are listening I say: Love your enemies, do good to those who hate you, bless those who curse you, pray for those who mistreat you. If someone slaps you on one cheek, turn to them the other also. If someone takes your coat, do not withhold your shirt from them."

What Jesus shares here is the kingdom of God at work in the world. "Give to anyone who asks from you, and if anyone takes what belongs to you, do not demand it back" (Luke 6:30). Jesus says we have no rights. The kingdom of God is founded on the principle that his people have no rights. Jesus gave up his rights. Philippians says it clearly: He took off the robe of royalty; he took off the robe of grandeur to walk among us. He clothed himself in humility. He emptied himself of his rights for our sakes (see Philippians 2:5–9).

What does Christ's kingdom look like then? It is a place where Christ alone is King and a place where his subjects trust his provision completely. It is a place where people are made one in him, regardless of family history or lineage, regardless of material wealth or poverty, regardless of education or the lack thereof. In this kingdom, Christ makes free those who were bound and uses his subjects to reach the "least of these" with his love and provision.

In his kingdom, there are no subjects more important than others, and he uses those who are blessed with more to reach those who have less. This is why I suggest that the kingdom of God and the will of God are bound together. And I believe this is why Jesus instructed us to pray, "Your kingdom come, you will be done," followed immediately by, "Give us today our daily bread." If bringing God's kingdom into our neighborhoods is *our* responsibility, it will certainly require *us* to trust God in a way that is not initially comfortable and that may even seem "unnatural" in our materialistic culture.

How can we give away to someone else what we have if we fear that this is all we have or will have? We won't! However, when we learn to truly trust God for our daily provision, we become free to do his will and to share all that we have with others who are in need.

As a Christian, there will likely come a time when you will be called to step out in faith in response to the leading of the Holy Spirit, and to do something for God that is beyond your human capacity or means. When God calls us to become "conduits he can flow through" rather than just "reservoirs he fills up," we will have to trust his provision.

> *When God calls us to become "conduits he can flow through" rather than just "reservoirs he fills up," we will have to trust his provision.*

Prayer that is communion with God is what will lead us into this kind of deep, unwavering trust. When our prayer life is communal rather than just petitionary, we can stand assured that God will supply our needs, and we can take that "leap of faith" without hesitation.

FACETS OF HIS GRACE:
A MOMENT OF FELLOWSHIP

Each of you should use whatever gift you have received to serve others, as faithful stewards of God's grace in its various forms. (1 Peter 4:10)

Pause and consider the multifaceted grace of God. God's grace—his unmerited favor—has been expressed to you in different ways or through various forms. Here are just a few:

- You have received God's grace through his abundant provision (see Philippians 4:19).
- You have received God's grace as he's shown you acceptance during those times when you've failed (see Romans 15:7).
- You have received God's grace when he's encouraged you when you were sad or disappointed (see 1 Thessalonians 5:11).
- You have received God's grace when he supported you during times of struggle (see Galatians 6:2).

Now pause and ask God, "How could I better give graciously and abundantly to others without fear?" Ask the Father to reveal a specific person who could benefit from receiving some of your material provisions. Ask him specifically about how to show more of his acceptance, encouragement, and support to others. Listen and be still. Allow God's Spirit to reveal the people in your life who need to receive more of his glorious grace expressed through you. After you've heard from the Lord, complete the following sentences.

Now that I have heard from the Lord,

- I could give some of my material provisions to _____.
- I could show more of God's acceptance to _____.
- I could give more of God's encouragement to _____.
- I could demonstrate more of God's support to _____.

"And let us consider how we may spur one another on toward love and good deeds" (Hebrews 10:24). With vulnerability and sincerity, share what God has revealed to you with a partner or small group. Pray together. Ask that God's Spirit would express his grace through you so that others would be able to see him in you. Offer a simple prayer, such as the following:

Heavenly Father, please help me to be more willing to give of my _____. Please show me how to do this in practical ways.

L2. *Listening to and hearing God for direction and discernment.*

Luke 6:31–32 states: "Do to others as you would have them do to you. If you love those who love you, what credit is that to you?" Oftentimes people say to me, "I love you," and I have been known to respond with, "I love you, too, but you are easy to love." Some people truly are easy to love. But what will we do about those who are difficult to love? Bringing the kingdom of God to this world involves loving not only those who are easy to love but also (especially!) loving those we find difficult to love. Jesus said even sinners love those who love them.

In the kingdom of God, everyone is loved. But what does this kingdom love really look like and what does it have to do with a lifestyle of prayer? If we are praying, "Give us today our daily bread," then we are learning to trust God for all our needs. This type of trust frees us to give graciously and bountifully to others without thought for what we might miss out on. We are learning to give without any need of receiving something in return.

> *This type of trust frees us to give graciously and bountifully to others without thought for what we might miss out on.*

Jesus said in Luke 6:34, "And if you lend to those from whom you expect repayment, what credit is that to you? Even sinners lend to sinners, expecting to be repaid in full." This is about much deeper issues than just money, just as "Give us today our daily bread" is about much deeper issues than food. It is about life.

"Love your enemies," Jesus tells us. "Do good to them, and lend to them without expecting to get anything back." (See Matthew 5:43-48.) We respond and say that this is preposterous. This is outrageous. There is not an economics professor in the world who would stand by this statement from Jesus. But Jesus calls the church to value that which seems contrary to our present culture. I know this is difficult, but Jesus calls the church to be different. He calls us to be the light shining in the darkness.

Luke 6 is tied to Matthew 6 in this: If I am willing to fully trust that God will provide for me, then I am able to give away every dime I have, not expecting repayment, because I know God is in charge of my money. God is in charge of my life as I give. Remember, this is not only about money; it's about giving away your life.

Luke 6:35 goes on to say, "But love your enemies, do good to them, and lend to them without expecting to get anything back. Then your reward will be great, and you will be children of the Most High." That's just like God. He gave to me when I had nothing to give him. He gives to me when I cannot repay him. He blesses me when I can do nothing for him. I want to be like him.

Then Jesus goes on to say:

> "Be merciful just as your Father is merciful.
>
> "Do not judge, and you will not be judged. Do not condemn, and you will not be condemned. Forgive, and you will be forgiven. Give, and it will be given to you. A good measure, pressed down, shaken together and running over, will be poured into your lap. For with the measure you use, it will be measured to you." (Luke 6:36–38)

When I trust God to provide for my every need, I become generous rather than selfish. Something happens in me when I trust God in this manner. When I surrender everything, something tremendous takes place in my life.

Listen to what Peter tells Jesus in Matthew 19:27: "We have left everything to follow you!" I love that Peter often says what everyone else is thinking. I am sure the other disciples were blown away by Peter's words. They probably said, "I can't believe he said that." And then, as an aside, they probably said, "Thank the Lord he said that." They all probably felt like Peter, in that they had left everything to follow Jesus.

Jesus was trying to teach them to totally trust him. He wanted them to be dependent on the Father. In the same way, God also wants *us* to be dependent upon him. Then Peter went on to say, "We have left everything to follow you! What then will there be for us?"

Jesus said to them, "Truly I tell you, at the renewal of all things …" (Matthew 19:28). This life is not all there is. You and I are here for only a short period of time. You can't keep what you have. When they put you in the grave, you'll take nothing with you. Since you can't keep your treasures here, why don't you send them on ahead? "Store up for yourselves treasures in heaven" (Matthew 6:20).

I am asking you to give away more than what is in your purse or your wallet. I'm asking you to give away your entire life to Jesus. He will take care of you. You will always get more from God than you give to him.

In Matthew 14:13–21, we find the story of a boy who participated in the work of the kingdom of God:

> When Jesus heard what had happened, he withdrew by boat privately to a solitary place. Hearing of this, the crowds followed him on foot from the towns. When Jesus landed and saw a large crowd, he had compassion on them and healed their sick.
>
> As evening approached, the disciples came to him and said, "This is a remote place, and it's already getting late. Send the crowds away, so they can go to the villages and buy themselves some food."
>
> Jesus replied, "They do not need to go away. You give them something to eat."

"We have here only five loaves of bread and two fish," they answered.

"Bring them here to me," he said. And he directed the people to sit down on the grass. Taking the five loaves and the two fish and looking up to heaven, he gave thanks and broke the loaves. Then he gave them to the disciples, and the disciples gave them to the people. They all ate and were satisfied, and the disciples picked up twelve basketfuls of broken pieces that were left over. The number of those who ate was about five thousand men, besides women and children.

When "Give us today our daily bread" is our prayer, and we link that together with the kingdom of God, we become like this little boy who was generous with what he had.

When you give God everything, he will always give you back more. Will you give everything to Jesus today? Will you participate in his kingdom, that kingdom which looks so different from the world? Will you trust him to provide your daily bread? Will you be broken for the world? Learning to live a life of conversation with God will enable us to trust him completely along the way.

Much like taking a walk with a person, as we walk close to God, we can always lean over to God and ask, "Is everything going to be alright?" And we can trust that he will always answer, "I love you, and I will take care of your needs." What a joy to have such a relationship with the Creator; that we can share conversation with him and trust his provision for us.

OPEN HANDS:
AN ENCOUNTER WITH JESUS

"Freely you have received; freely give." (Matthew 10:8)

There is no better illustration of freely receiving and freely giving of God's provision than Christ's miracle of feeding thousands. Pause quietly to picture this image of Jesus. His eyes are focused toward heaven as he recognizes the source of all provision. His hands are open, to both give and to receive. With one hand, he receives what is available—five loaves and two fish from a young boy; with the other hand, he gives freely and abundantly to the needs of others.

The Savior asks the same of us today. At times, his calling is to freely receive what he gives to you. At other times, he calls you to freely give to meet the needs of others. But remember that his inheritance toward you never runs out; his provision is without limits.

Now quietly consider what encouragement, care, support, or affirmation you might need in the midst of your struggles? Yield to the Holy Spirit within you. Open your heart to receive these gifts from Christ, the one who provides.

Jesus, as I look at the circumstances and challenges of my life, I need to receive more of your _____. Could you speak to me about how you want to provide? With one hand, I am looking to you for _____.

Finally, what acceptance, compassion, appreciation, resource, or respect might you freely give to someone this week? Could you take the time to think of a specific name and then yield to the Spirit's prompting? As you share his life and love, others will find hope in the Jesus who provides.

Jesus, as I look at the people who are in my life today, I know I am called to give. Who needs to receive from me? With my other hand, I'm asking you to empower me to give to _____ so he/she can experience hope in you.

L3. *Experiencing God as he really is through deepened intimacy with him.*

Chapter 4

Prayer as Participation in the Kingdom of God

I want to warn you: What I am going to share next from God's Word won't be easy to accept. In fact, we might as well say that to carry out these next instructions from Jesus concerning prayer, we will need a supernatural outpouring of the power of the Holy Spirit. What Jesus requires of all those who would follow him is 100 percent abandonment and trust.

When we read the Word of God, it's important to look for key phrases. There was one that Jesus often used, that whenever we see or hear it, we should take note. What is that phrase? "The kingdom of heaven." When we hear Jesus say in Scripture, "The kingdom of heaven" or, "The kingdom of heaven is like" or if he ends his statement with "This is the kingdom of heaven," then we should prepare ourselves to be both shocked and challenged. In a kingdom there must always be a king, and the ruler of the kingdom of heaven is the King of kings, Jesus. Therefore, when we consider the kingdom of heaven, we can describe it as the complete rule of Christ, not in a single place but in our hearts.

Jesus used the kingdom-of-heaven language so we could understand what he was calling us to be and do. His kingdom is not of this world. We must remember that we are not, in fact, citizens of this world either; we are only strangers here. In a sense, we have been given a worker's visa to be in this world, to temporarily work here. We are not from here; we are citizens of the kingdom of heaven. We do not belong to this culture. We do not belong to this world's kingdoms. We have no rights in this culture. We are simply here to give witness to the kingdom of God to which we belong.

The principles Jesus shares with us are not the principles of this world, but of another world. He challenges us to be something other than what this earthly world wants us to be. He is sharing with us a way of being in the world that will challenge us to give ourselves away for the sake of this world.

He is sharing with us a way of being in the world that will challenge us to give ourselves away for the sake of this world.

We have been looking at the Lord's Prayer. In Luke 11:1, the disciples said to Jesus, "Teach us to pray." In response, Jesus answered them: "This, then, is how you should pray" (Matthew 6:9). We've been considering five sections of the Lord's Prayer. Of these five sections, the fourth section—which is the one we're discussing now—is the only place in the Lord's prayer where Jesus gives extra commentary. Most likely, this is because he knows it will be the most difficult part for us to accept.

Jesus said, in Matthew 6:12–13, "And forgive us our debts, as we also have forgiven our debtors. And lead us not into temptation, but deliver us from the evil one." Then Jesus adds a bit of additional commentary in verses 14–15: "For if you forgive other people when they sin against you, your heavenly Father will also forgive you. But if you do not forgive others their sins, your Father will not forgive your sins."

Remember, as we have noted all along, Jesus is not teaching the disciples how to pray in a single, momentary event; rather, he is teaching them how to pray through all of life—to pray as a lifestyle. We commune with God as our Father, and we know he will supply our needs. We have accepted that the will of God and the kingdom of God are intermingled. We cannot pray, "God, let your will be done in my life," without praying, "Lord, this all relates to the kingdom."

Moving on to part four, as we pray, "Help us forgive others as we have been forgiven," we see three aspects of forgiveness. First, Jesus makes it obvious that those in his kingdom are called to forgive others. Our communion with the Father is affected by our relationship with his children. Praying this type of prayer—"Father, forgive me as I forgive others"—is critical, as it may reveal unforgiveness in us.

Prayer is essential because in prayer we come to know God more fully, and we come to know who we truly are. Jesus speaks of this kind of communion with God in Matthew 5:23–24: "Therefore, if you are offering your gift at the altar and there remember that your brother or sister has something against you, leave your gift there in front of the altar. First go and be reconciled to them; then come and offer your gift."

Prayer is essential because in prayer we come to know God more fully, and we come to know who we truly are.

FREEDOM AND FORGIVENESS:
AN ENCOUNTER WITH JESUS

You, my brothers and sisters, were called to be free. But do not use your freedom to indulge the flesh; rather, serve one another humbly in love. (Galatians 5:13)

Pause for the next moments, and have your own time of communion with God. Pray the following kind of prayer:

Heavenly Father, show me your forgiveness. Reveal the ways and specific times when I have received your forgiveness. Remind me of how your forgiveness has benefited me. I also ask that you reveal the true character of my heart. How am I doing at sharing your forgiveness with others?

Continue your prayer, like King David's prayer in Psalm 51:10:

Create in me a pure heart, Father. Search me and know my heart. Show me the ways I have withheld your forgiveness from others. Give me a heart that's willing to forgive.

Next, reflect on a recent time in your life when you struggled to forgive someone. Share your thoughts with Jesus. Tell him about your sadness and regret.

Lord, I know that I did not love well recently when _____.
Father, I know that I've struggled to forgive _____.

Now prepare for a time of cleansing and renewal with Jesus:

Lord, by your Spirit, would you remove anything from my life that hinders the expression of your love? Cleanse me, forgive me, and empower me to forgive others and love like Jesus forgave and loved.

L5. *Living with a passionate longing for purity and to please him in all things.*

If you are offering a gift at the altar, who are you offering your gift to? You are offering it to God. You are offering your gift at the altar and there you remember! Prayer says, "Reveal to me who you are, God, and show me who I am!" You say, "Lord, I've come to pray; I offer you my gift. I've come to surrender myself to you," and you *remember* what the Scripture says.

This is a holy remembering that only comes through the working and operating of the Holy Spirit. As you are there in communion with God, the Holy Spirit speaks to you, and you remember that your brother or sister has something against you. You *remember* that Jesus said, "Leave your gift there, in front of the altar. First go and be reconciled to them; then come and offer your gift."

Our prayer time and communion with God is affected by our communion with others. If I come to commune with God and there is something between someone else and me, God will not allow me to continue in deep communion with him until I have made things right.

> *Our prayer time and communion with God is affected by our communion with others. If I come to commune with God and there is something between someone else and me, God will not allow me to continue in deep communion with him until I have made things right.*

I know people, and you probably know people too (maybe you are one of those people!), who can hold something against someone for years. As followers of Jesus Christ, we are seeking a deeper communion with Christ. We desire for God to remove anything in us that may harm that communion.

In my pastoral ministry that has spanned over twenty-five years, I have seen many people who have a deep longing to walk with Christ. I've ministered to people who say they have a vibrant prayer life. Many have told me that God speaks to them, that God knows everything about them. They tell me, "I'm walking in the Spirit." However, If I see that person locked in a bitter battle with someone else, I don't know how they can have a vibrant prayer life and walk in the Spirit—because I can't. God won't allow me.

God has never allowed me to hold grudges against others and battle them, holding on to hard feelings, while spending time in communion with God. We cannot love God and hate people, regardless of what they may have done to us, or those we love. Time with God transforms and melts our hearts toward others, even those who may have hurt us.

God issues challenges to me when I'm at the altar (both

privately and in a corporate setting) in communion with him. I can't get past that thing. He says, "Stop. There's something there. Let's fix that. Go offer yourself. Go surrender yourself. Go repair whatever is wrong between you and that person."

I remember a time when I was seeking God. It was my desire to be closer to him. I wanted to walk in the power of the Holy Spirit; I wanted to encounter God in a new way. As I was praying and fasting, God began to reveal people in my life whom I had hurt through unkind actions. I deeply appreciated God showing me these issues because I wanted to make them right. I wanted to say I was sorry for acting in a way that displeased God and for hurting someone else.

I felt like I could go and ask forgiveness, and I felt like God would go with me. After all, it was his idea for me to ask forgiveness, so I believed it would work out, and with God's help I was always able to ask for forgiveness from those who were hurt. This, however, is not the end of the story or the end of the words that God wanted to speak to me as I endeavored to draw closer to him in prayer. This was only the beginning.

God began to deal with me about what seemed to be a much longer list. The Holy Spirit reminded me of others who had hurt me and my family. Suddenly, this was not about people I had injured, but about people who had injured me. God brought them to my attention through prayer. He didn't bring them up to stir up old, hurtful feelings; rather, he brought them to my mind because there were people in my life I had not fully forgiven. He revealed them to me—their names and faces.

There I was—I wanted to be like Jesus more than anything in the world. And Jesus showed me something that was keeping me from becoming more like him—unforgiveness. So he revealed to me all the people I was still struggling to forgive. To be honest, I had come to believe I had forgiven everyone who'd hurt me. That's precisely why prayer—conversation with God—is so important in our lives.

Our prayer lives cannot become "one-way" communication with the Father. We must be willing to listen as well as speak. I was trying to listen to what the Holy Spirit was saying. There were two questions that were important to me as he was speaking: "Will I be able to listen?" and, "Will I be able to respond?" All those people I thought I had forgiven were brought to my mind when I brought my gift to him at the altar. When I thought I had given him everything, God revealed to me that there was more I needed to release.

As I was seeking God about these people, he spoke to me again and said, "A great way to judge how much I have transformed you is to see how you react to the failure of your enemies." As citizens in the kingdom of God, we are not called to hatred. We're not called to be against our enemies.

What was God saying to me? Was it true that I had unforgiveness in my heart toward people who had deeply wounded me? Was this secret unforgiveness affecting my communion with him? Perhaps God is asking you to search your own heart today. Is it possible that you may have some unforgiveness in your heart as well, which is affecting your conversation with God?

How do you feel about that certain someone who hurt you so long ago? How do you feel when you hear of them hurting, falling, or failing? Let's say someone who has hurt you in the past, maybe who stole something from you or hurt your family, loses his or her job. Do you feel good on the inside to see him or her in that position? Do you say, "That's right, God! He deserves that. I hope he loses everything because he deserves it."? If you're having those kinds of reactions, then you may need to pray for a deeper transformation. You may need to offer a bit of forgiveness of your own. The kingdom of God requires us to love everyone and forgive everyone, regardless of what they have done to us. In our times of conversation with God, he reveals these wounds to us so that we can be healed. Proverbs 24:17–18 reminds us, "Do not gloat when your enemy falls; when they stumble, do not let your heart rejoice, or the LORD will see and disapprove and turn his wrath away from them."

There is a fact that I've learned the hard way over time: We can't make everyone love or forgive us. They must choose to do so. We shouldn't get overly upset when people don't do what we think they should. We are simply called to offer ourselves to them. We can say, "Here I am—I'm sorry."

Life in the kingdom requires us to surrender ourselves in this manner because we are witnesses to the kingdom of heaven in this world. This may not be easy, but with the Spirit's help it can be done. If we are following the will of God, we can be assured that he will go with us.

Mark 11:22–24 says:

> "Have faith in God," Jesus answered. "Truly I tell you, if anyone says to this mountain, 'Go, throw yourself into

the sea,' and does not doubt in their heart but believes that what they say will happen, it will be done for them. Therefore I tell you, whatever you ask for in prayer, believe that you have received it, and it will be yours."

What amazing power God has bestowed upon us, that we can say to a mountain, "Be removed," and it will be removed! We can become powerful people of prayer.

That's why you are reading this book, right? You and I want to be people who practice prevailing prayer. We want to have a lifestyle of deep communion with God. However, God doesn't let us stop there. This passage in Mark is not just about throwing mountains aside. There is more. Certainly, he says, "Throw that mountain aside; curse that fig tree." But Jesus also says, "As you stand praying (for that mountain to be removed), if you hold anything against anyone," then you must respond to the Spirit's direction.

In Matthew 5:23–24, Jesus speaks about others holding on to offenses against us. But here, Jesus says, "If *you* hold anything against anyone, forgive them." In my understanding of what Jesus is saying, before we can cast any mountains into a sea, we must first deal with the unforgiveness in our heart.

We cannot do this in and of ourselves. This can only happen through the supernatural work of the Holy Spirit. Don't despair, for God is here with you. Don't despair, for you are not alone. Don't despair, for you've not been asked to do anything he will not enable you to do. Those in the kingdom are called to forgive and God will make that possible.

MOVE THE MOUNTAIN:
AN EXPERIENCE OF SCRIPTURE

"If you remain in me and my words remain in you, ask whatever you wish, and it will be done for you." (John 15:7)

Pause in bold belief, asking God to reveal the person of Jesus to you. Ask him to show you how he is the one who is humble and gentle and able to teach you how to forgive (see Matthew 11:28–29). Ask the Spirit to reveal Jesus as the one who forgives and calls us to do the same (see Ephesians 5:31–32). Ask the Father to reveal the "mountains" he wants you to be able to move, beginning with any unforgiveness that may be in your heart.

Father, I want to see and encounter the person of Jesus. I know your Word is living and active, so do a work in me so that I have your humility, your gentleness, and your holiness. Change me so that I might join you in forgiving others as I have been forgiven. I come before you with confidence and boldness, claiming the promise that you have heard me and will answer me. Show me the mountains you want me to move and the next steps of faith you have for me (see Hebrews 4:14; John 15:7).

L8. *Disciplined, bold, and believing prayer.*

The second point God wants to speak to us regarding forgiveness is this: There is a place in the church for repentance.

Repentance is not only for people outside the church; repentance is what should happen inside the church too. The way of the kingdom is through the cross.

I would like to draw your attention to the cross for a moment. Notice what the gospel writer Luke describes in chapter 23. We picture Jesus hanging between two criminals:

> Two other men, both criminals, were also led out with him to be executed. When they came to the place called the Skull, they crucified him there, along with the criminals—one on his right, the other on his left. Jesus said, "Father, forgive them, for they do not know what they are doing." (Luke 23:32–34)

They beat him severely—"Father, forgive them." They nailed him to a cross—"Father, forgive them." They divided up his clothes and cast lots for them—"Father, forgive them." They didn't know what they were doing—"Father, forgive them." I know this is difficult, but we see on the cross the Son of God who is saying, "Forgive them!" The way of the kingdom is through the cross.

I've heard many people say, "I will forgive them, but I will never forget." I've also heard people say, "I will remember what they did to me until the day I die." That is exactly right—in and of yourself, you will most likely remember. But you can die to yourself today. Thank God you can surrender yourself to Jesus on the cross and he can transform your life.

Those old feelings can be transformed. You can be reborn in Jesus Christ. What is impossible to forget on your own can be erased by the power of the Holy Spirit. You can be freed from the stronghold of old emotional wounds. Through the love and power of the Holy Spirit, you can not only forgive, but you can also forget. This will only happen through the grace of the Spirit—but it *can* happen.

> *Old feelings can be transformed—you can be reborn in Jesus Christ. What is impossible to forget on your own can be erased by the power of the Holy Spirit.*

Forgiveness is not only an intellectual or mental exercise; it is spiritual transformation. If you are going to forgive those who have bruised you, who have hurt you, who have crushed you, it will require the power of the Holy Spirit in your life.

HE MUST INCREASE:
A MOMENT OF FELLOWSHIP

He must become greater; I must become less. (John 3:30)

This passage of Scripture reveals a critical ingredient to living a life of prevailing prayer: True repentance brings a two-dimensional imperative—he must increase and I must decrease! This imperative is not just for John the Baptist, but for each Spirit-empowered follower of Jesus Christ.

Practically, what does it look like for Jesus to gain prominence in our lives? What does it look like for him to increase as we decrease? Think about your daily living, your thoughts and activities, your attitudes and priorities. Scripture reminds us that:

- His perspective and his ways are different from our ways (see Isaiah 55:8).
- His activity is characterized by the fruit of the Spirit, like love, peace, patience, kindness, gentleness, and self-control. He never relates with us according to the deeds of the flesh (see Galatians 5:19–23).
- His heart is characterized by humility and thinking more highly of others, offering forgiveness and grace (see Philippians 2:3).

As Jesus continues to increase and we continue to decrease, every part of our lives will be impacted.

Pause and reflect on these sentences. Talk with another person or share with your small group. Celebrate any evidence of how Jesus is increasing and how you are dying to self.

- I was recently prompted to consider my unforgiveness. I now see more of the Lord's perspective and was able to show forgiveness in a relationship by _____.
- Recently, I sensed the Spirit's work in me as I showed more love/patience/kindness/gentleness toward _____. I died a little more in my own attitude of _____.
- It was Christ's attitude of humility displayed in me recently, when _____. By his Spirit, I could think more highly of others by _____.

Celebrate one or more of these evidences of Christ's increasing presence in your life, and then pray for one another. Pray that these changes will continue and that each of you will live a life of prevailing prayer.

L9. *Yielding to the Spirit's fullness as life in the Spirit brings gifts and witness of the fruit of the Spirit.*

Peter asked Jesus a question in Matthew 18:21, a question that you and I should ask as people in this world. Remember, we are in this world, but we are not of this world. We're a part of the kingdom of God. We are only strangers here. We have cultural differences—we even speak with different accents!

When I was sixteen years old, I preached my first set of services in at a revival meeting in Indiana. Indiana is not too far north ("up north" is what we called it), but it was much further north than Alabama, where I was from. When I went there to preach, several people were so enamored with the way I spoke that they would ask me to say something again. I'm sure it wasn't because they couldn't understand me but because they wanted to hear the way I said the words again, in a slow, drawn-out way. There was a definite difference in the way I spoke and the way they spoke. We were speaking the same language, but the cultural nuances of that language were easily perceptible. It was easy for them to identify me as a "foreigner" because I spoke differently.

In the same manner, we should be easily identifiable as we live in this fallen world, because we are citizens of a different culture. Because we are citizens of the kingdom of heaven, there should be perceptible differences in the way we live our daily lives. Offering grace and forgiveness to those who do us wrong should be a defining characteristic of those who follow Jesus:

> Then Peter came to Jesus and he asked, "Lord, how many times shall I forgive my brother or sister who sins against me? Up to seven times?"
>
> Jesus answered, "I tell you, not seven times, but seventy-seven times.

"Therefore the kingdom of heaven is like …" (Matthew 18:21–23)

Whoa, that's a rough phrase! Jesus is challenging us who are citizens of the kingdom of heaven to forgive often and to forgive repeatedly:

> "Therefore, the kingdom of heaven is like a king who wanted to settle accounts with his servants. As he began the settlement, a man who owed him ten thousand bags of gold was brought to him. Since he was not able to pay, the master ordered that he and his wife and his children and all that he had be sold to repay the debt.
>
> "At this the servant fell on his knees before him. 'Be patient with me,' he begged, 'and I will pay back everything.' The servant's master took pity on him, canceled the debt and let him go.
>
> But when that servant went out, he found one of his fellow servants who owed him a hundred silver coins. He grabbed him and began to choke him. 'Pay back what you owe me!' he demanded.
>
> His fellow servant fell to his knees and begged him, 'Be patient with me, and I will pay it back.'" (Matthew 18:23–29)

When I reach this point of the story, I wonder why this man didn't recall his previous experiences, when he begged for his master to forgive him for all the gold he owed! It is in times of prayer and conversation with God, when we are begging for mercy, that he reveals to us those moments when we have not given mercy. Jesus continued the story:

"But he refused. Instead, he went off and had the man thrown into prison until he could pay the debt. When the other servants saw what had happened, they were outraged and went and told their master everything that had happened.

Then the master called the servant in. 'You wicked servant,' he said, 'I canceled all that debt of yours because you begged me to.'" (Matthew 18:30–32)

We need to remember how God listened when we begged for forgiveness:

"'Shouldn't you have had mercy on your fellow servant just as I had on you?' In anger his master handed him over to the jailers to be tortured, until he should pay back all he owed.

"This is how my heavenly Father will treat each of you unless you forgive your brother or sister from your heart." (Matthew 18:33–35)

These are not my words; they are Jesus' words. The enduring reality of the kingdom of God is that God requires us to be in right standing with our brothers and sisters in order to be in right standing with him. Our prayer life is greatly affected by our relationship with others.

Not only are we called to forgive, not only does the way of the kingdom go through the cross, but here is the third point: God's forgiveness transforms me to forgive.

This would be a bleak and hard message if the only part you remember is, "I have to forgive. I am required to forgive those who have hurt me, those who have bruised me, those who have hurt my family."

Jesus told Nicodemus:

"Very truly I tell you, no one can see the kingdom of God"—no one can see, no one can comprehend, no one can understand what it means to be in the kingdom of God—"unless they have been born again."

"How can someone be born when they are old?" Nicodemus asked. "Surely they cannot enter a second time into their mother's womb to be born!"

Jesus answered, "Very truly I tell you, no one can enter the kingdom of God unless they are born of water and the Spirit. Flesh gives birth to flesh, but the Spirit gives birth to spirit." (John 3:3–6)

Sometimes when I read what Jesus says throughout the Gospels, I feel as if Jesus slapped me right in the face! The words of Jesus will squeeze us; they pressure us. They drive us to him.

It has been said that what is in us is revealed by pressure. When we squeeze an orange, we find out what is inside it. Likewise, when we get squeezed in life, it reveals what's inside of us. When we're hard-pressed on every side, we quickly realize how deep (or shallow) we've gone in our relationship with Christ. Jesus' forgiveness transforms us to be able to forgive others. When you are born again, when you are reborn of the Spirit, you change your citizenship, you are a different person, you are part of a different kingdom. And Jesus' forgiveness transforms you to forgive.

Unforgiveness is a prison. I know how difficult it can be. There is so much hurt and so much pain in the world today. Oftentimes, it's not merely our pain, but the pain of a loved one for which we harbor unforgiveness. We long for the Holy Spirit to cause the presence and power of Jesus Christ to become alive in us so we can react to pain and suffering as Jesus did on the cross: "Father, forgive them."

The enemy holds you captive if you are in the prison of unforgiveness. But Jesus said, "The Spirit of the Lord is on me, because he has anointed me to proclaim good news to the poor. He has sent me to proclaim freedom" (Luke 4:18). Childish prayers ask for revenge; they want God to punish those who have hurt us or those we love. But a transformed person, a mature person, a person who has died and been reborn, will go to his knees and say, "Father, forgive them."

"Lord, I commune with you as my Father. Hallowed be your name. I praise you; I worship you. Your kingdom come, your will be done, on earth as it is in heaven. I surrender everything in my own life for your kingdom's sake. I trust that you will supply my needs. Give me this day my daily bread. And forgive me as I forgive those who have wronged me."

I was blessed to enjoy a good childhood. Some of you reading these words may have not had a good childhood. I don't pretend to know what it would mean to forgive someone who abused me. I do not know how it feels to be wronged to that degree, or to have been molested or physically hurt. I don't claim to know what it's like to go through a bad home life, a bad family situation, difficult friendships, or a mean and hateful supervisor at work. I cannot tell you that God is going to wave a magic wand and instantly fix everything. However, I can tell you that Jesus understands your hurt and pain, and he is willing to restore your heart as you commune with him.

I challenge you today to bring your pain to the cross and let God do a work in you that will begin to unlock you from your prison of unforgiveness. Let God do what only God can do. He is the only one who can free us. It's funny how we harbor those feelings against someone else and we're the only ones who are suffering. His forgiveness transforms me to be able to forgive others. "Father, forgive me as I forgive others."

Forgiveness will free you. Forgiveness will transform you. Forgiveness will enliven you. Forgiveness will change you for the better. Forgiveness will make you more like Christ. Pray now that you can release any unforgiveness in your life. Give it to God today. His hands are outstretched. He's waiting on you.

HE IS YOUR ADVOCATE:
AN EXPERIENCE OF SCRIPTURE

"When the Advocate comes, whom I will send to you from the Father—the Spirit of truth who goes out from the Father—he will testify about me." (John 15:26)

Take the next few moments and ask the Holy Spirit to be your Advocate for forgiveness and freedom. Ask him to reveal *more of Jesus* as you reflect on the needs of your life and the circumstances of your world. What needs and challenges are you facing where he can empower your forgiveness, healing, and hope?

Now ask the Holy Spirit to testify about the character of Jesus. Does the Spirit want you to know that Jesus is the All-Powerful One, the Mighty Counselor, or the Comforter? Does he want you to be reminded that he is the God of restoration and the ultimate provider of grace and forgiveness? One of the Spirit's functions is to reveal to you more of Jesus.

Holy Spirit, given the needs of my life and the challenges I face, what do you want to share with me about Jesus? What do you want me to know about him?

Listen as the Spirit testifies about Jesus. Yield to the Spirit's prompting to forgive, to heal, and to renew hope.

SPIRIT-
EMPOWERED
Faith

L2. *Listening to and hearing God for direction and discernment.*

Chapter 5

Victorious Life through Prayer

So far in *Conversation with God*, we've examined how we could use the Lord's Prayer as a model for our personal prayer life and developing a lifestyle of conversation with God. We've been working our way through the Lord's Prayer. But rather than calling it the Lord's Prayer, we could call it the Disciples' Prayer because it was given in answer to the disciples' request for Jesus to teach them how to pray. Jesus answered, telling them, and thereby us:

> "This, then, is how you should pray: 'Our Father in heaven, hallowed be your name, your kingdom come, your will be done, on earth as it is in heaven. Give us today our daily bread. And forgive us our debts, as we also have forgiven our debtors. And lead us not into temptation, but deliver us from the evil one.'" (Matthew 6:9–13)

When the disciples asked Jesus, "Teach us to pray," they weren't asking for a specific form of prayer; rather, they wanted to know how to engage in a life of prayer—a life of unbroken communion with the Father—the same type of communion Jesus enjoyed. These aspects of the Lord's instructions have become more important than a responsive reading type prayer (not that this is wrong). They have become more than keys to successful praying or a way that we always get our prayers answered. We can pray in the way that Jesus has instructed us to pray and live and perceive God not only as Lord, not only as King, but as our loving, heavenly Father.

We come to God in prayer in a lifestyle of praise for his goodness and his provision. We acknowledge that to praise God for his goodness, his love and his mercy, his personality and his nature, is a wonderful addition to praising God for what he has done. God is worthy to be praised for his nature and his attributes as much as for his gifts and blessings. If we are in the habit of praising God only for what he does for us, we may be tempted to be thankful only for what we can see him do in our lives. In God's nature and personality of love and goodness, he always has our best interests in mind. He is always motivated by his love for us.

We've learned to pray, "Your kingdom come," and, "Your will be done," together. We cannot separate God's will for our lives from the work that builds his kingdom. His kingdom is one of love, forgiveness, selflessness, and submission. Saying, "Your will be done in my life," carries the weight of forgiveness and selflessness and submission to the kingdom of God.

FULLNESS OF LIFE:
AN EXPERIENCE OF SCRIPTURE

"I have come that they may have life, and have it to the full." (John 10:10)

Ask God to bring you into such intimacy and closeness with him that a rich, satisfying life and bold witness are the result. Ask him for a life of forgiveness, selflessness, and submission to the kingdom of God.

Father God, with a grateful heart I cling to your promise. Hearing Christ's promise of a full and abundant life gives me security and hope. Open the eyes of my heart so that I can draw closer to you each day. I want to see your plans for yieldedness, selflessness, forgiveness, submission, and bold witness through my life.

L10. *Practicing the presence of the Lord, yielding to the Spirit's work of Christlikeness.*

In prayer, we have learned to trust our Father as our provider and to live in a state of communion with him, continually trusting that he will guide us and help us. I cannot possibly hope to surrender to his will if I do not trust him as my sustainer and provider. If he sees every sparrow that falls to the ground, he sees every need that you and I have.

Now we come to this part in the Lord's Prayer, which many may not understand: "Lead us not into temptation" (Matthew 6:10). The New Living Translation renders it as, "Don't let us yield to temptation."

There are many Christians today who are not walking victoriously in their relationship with Christ because they are struggling with habitual sin. Many people have come to accept Jesus as their Savior; they have trusted him as Lord and asked him to forgive their sins. Many people have made a "profession of faith," which is wonderful.

However, the type of battle Jesus is speaking of when he is instructing us to pray is not a small battle. It is a battle over evil, over sin, and over temptation. This battle cannot be won with a simple profession of faith or by mere willpower. This battle is won only by his power, and it is the work of the Holy Spirit in the life of the believer that produces victory over sin.

> *The battle Jesus speaks of when instructing us to pray is a battle over evil, over sin, and over temptation.*

Am I saying that when we come to Christ and allow him to redeem us and transform (sanctify) us, that we will never commit sin again? No! But neither am I saying that it's the will of God to continue to sin (disobey him). What I am saying is that though we may not be able to say we will *never* sin, we have been transformed so we don't *have* to continue to sin. We are no longer compelled to sin, but we are now compelled to live holy through the power of the Holy Spirit in Christ Jesus.

We are walking after God, but we recognize we are in a battle to fully surrender to all that Christ wants to accomplish in and through us. The Gospel of Matthew describes the battle Jesus fought through prayer in the garden of Gethsemane:

Going a little farther, he fell with his face to the ground and prayed, "My Father, if it is possible, may this cup be taken from me. Yet not as I will, but as you will."

Then he returned to his disciples and found them sleeping. "Couldn't you men keep watch with me for one hour?" he asked Peter. "Watch and pray so that you will not fall into temptation. The spirit is willing, but the flesh is weak." (Matthew 26:39–41)

The flesh, as the Scripture often describes it, could be defined as the desires we are born into this world with: desires to please ourselves, desires to do things our own way, even if it means destroying ourselves.

When the Scripture speaks of operating in the Spirit, it can be defined as that move, unction, or working of the transformational power of God that changes our desires. When we say we are operating in the Spirit, it's the working of God's Holy Spirit that changes our desires from selfish to selfless. He opens our hearts to the working, the loving, and the moving of the Holy Spirit, thus enabling us to experience the refreshing waters of his Spirit.

The phrase, "Lead us not into temptation," speaks of being tempted by our enemy, satan, who is coming against us with all manner of evil opportunities. As I prayed over and prepared this teaching, I fought a sense of fear. In my study, the Lord spoke to me about victory over sin. A life of temptation can overtake us, but God can lead us to victory over sin. My fear came from the idea that if I am going to share that we can have victory over sin, just as surely as I do that, all hell will come against me. So I said, "Lord, keep me. Make me walk in victory over sin."

"Lead us not into temptation," speaks of the reality that satan comes against us with opportunities to sin. Sin is defined as disobedience to God's desire for your life. Satan offering us an opportunity or a temptation to sin is exactly what Jesus is telling us to pray about. Sin seeks to destroy the Christian. When we sin, we are essentially submitting to the works of satan. This has been described in Scripture at times as the "defilement of flesh and spirit" (2 Corinthians 7:1 NASB). It thwarts God's ideal plan for our lives.

If we say, "Why are you preaching about sin? I'm walking in grace," surely, we mean then that God's grace is keeping us from sin. Engaging through prayer to be victorious over sin is critical in our journey toward spiritual maturity. Sin is a separator, separating us from God. Sin destroys and deadens our ability to hear God's voice. Sin, or disobeying God's will for our lives, creates barriers between God and us.

One of the functions of the Holy Spirit, according to Jesus, is to "prove the world to be in the wrong about sin and righteousness and judgement" (John 16:8). The Spirit works in us to enable us to see the reality of where we are in Christ and reveal to us possible areas of disobedience and our need for continued surrender to God. As believers we learn to listen for the voice of the Holy Spirit as he reveals to us our areas of weakness. We must become familiar with the voice of the Holy Spirit, desiring the power of Pentecost in our lives. Our desire is to become familiar enough with the voice of the Holy Spirit that we immediately recognize when he says yes and when he says no. We need to be familiar enough that we know it is him telling us, "That's not right for you," or, "You've drifted too far."

Sin is a destroyer. Jesus has come into our lives; it is him we are serving. Yet we seem to be consistently subjected to failure, subjected to the continued stronghold of sin. You may live in a place of constant failure or sin. Following a weekly worship service, you may feel good and feel as if you've left your burden at the altar, only to leave the church building and find that you are still trapped in the stronghold of sin. We are in a spiritual battle for our very souls!

SET ME FREE:
AN ENCOUNTER WITH JESUS

"If you hold to my teaching, you are really my disciples. Then you will know the truth, and the truth will set you free." (John 8:31–32)

In the gospel of John, Jesus reveals how we can experience deepened transformation in Christlikeness and victory in this battle against sin and the flesh. Encountering Jesus in Scripture transforms us into his likeness, empowering our life of prevailing prayer:

- Truth cannot be subjectively created; truth is and comes from the objective, absolute person of Christ. As John wrote: "For the law was given through Moses, but grace and truth came through Jesus Christ" (John 1:17).

- Truth cannot be relative and change from person to person, from community to community, because Jesus is the incarnation of the God "with whom there is no variation or shifting shadow" (James 1:17 NASB). As the Scripture says: "Jesus Christ is the same yesterday and today and forever" (Hebrews 13:8).
- All proclaimed truth cannot be equal, because Jesus didn't claim to be "a truth," one that is equal to all others. His claim was exclusive. He claimed to be the One and only truth, the only way to God. "Jesus said to him, 'I am the way, the truth, and the life. No one comes to the Father except through me'" (John 14:6). Those are not the words of someone who is one among many, someone who is equal to all others. Those are the words of one who has no equal:

I am the Lord, and there is no other;
  apart from me there is no God.
I will strengthen you,
  though you have not acknowledged me,
so that from the rising of the sun
  to the place of its setting
  people may know there is none besides me.
  I am the Lord, and there is no other.
(Isaiah 45:5–6)

Pause and reflect on areas of your life that have potential for growth and change as you embrace specific truth from Scripture. Where could spiritual awakening take place in your life as you walk in the light of God's Word?

Dear Lord, please search me thoroughly and help me to become aware of sins in my life that are hindering my intimacy with you and kingdom witness. What truth from the Word do you want me to embrace so that I might experience more of your freedom from sin and better express Jesus? Speak to me, Lord. your servant is listening.

L3. *Experiencing God as he really is through deepened intimacy with him.*

Many people have said it's a harder battle once you make a commitment to walk with Christ. They will even say, "My life was easy and good until I decided to follow Jesus." I've heard that many times. The reason many people feel this way is that the forces of evil have ramped up their onslaught against them.

As Jesus was speaking to his disciples about this spiritual battle, he spoke to Peter, calling him by his original name: "Simon, Simon, Satan has asked to sift all of you as wheat" (Luke 22:31). The picture I see Jesus painting for Peter here is that satan was out to destroy him. Jesus continues, "But I have prayed for you, Simon, that your faith may not fail. And when you have turned back, strengthen your brothers" (Luke 22:32). I am sure there is an enemy of my soul who's out to destroy me, who wants to see me fall, but I'm also sure that Jesus Christ, who sits at the right hand of God the Father, is making intercession for me, praying that I would not fail (see Romans 8:34).

Surely Peter's heart was penetrated with the words of Jesus. In 1 Peter 5:8–9, Peter says to the church:

> Be alert and of sober mind. Your enemy the devil prowls around like a roaring lion looking for someone to

devour. Resist him, standing firm in the faith, because you know that the family of believers throughout the world is undergoing the same kind of sufferings.

It becomes clear that the battle with sin is not something to be played with, although many Christians take this battle lightly. If you are a Christian and are continuing to practice sin because you think you are under grace, you are playing a dangerous game with your soul.

We seek to understand what it is that Jesus is encouraging us to pray for: The power to overcome the temptation to sin and not fall away or not fall out of the will of God. It is possible that some of you were tempted heavily even this week. It's possible you were tempted, even today, to be disobedient to God's will and God's plan for your life.

James seeks to help us understand how God's transformative power will keep us in the hour of temptation:

Blessed is the one who perseveres under trial because, having stood the test, that person will receive the crown of life that the Lord has promised to those who love him.

When tempted, no one should say, "God is tempting me." For God cannot be tempted by evil, nor does he tempt anyone; but each person is tempted when they are dragged away by their own evil desire and enticed. Then, after desire has conceived, it gives birth to sin; and sin, when it is full-grown, gives birth to death. (James 1:12–15)

In this passage, we see a description of the heat of the battle. James tells us that the person is tempted when he or she is dragged away by his or her own evil desire. The question we can ask is this: "What is it that I desire?"

We can imagine satan as a fisherman with a hook—not a simple hook, but a treble hook with three prongs and sharp barbs. Satan's hook is not like a straight pin that could easily be pull out if it pierced your skin; his hook has barbs that press into your flesh and will not let go easily. Satan does not say, "Here's the hook—there's no danger." No, satan is known as the master of disguise.

The enemy disguises that hook of sin. Just as any good fisherman knows which bait to cast for each type of fish, so satan knows what will work against us. When I was a boy, both of my grandfathers had fishing ponds on their farms. When I went fishing in those ponds, I would take two types of bait with me: chicken livers and worms. Neither of those things sound appealing to me, but my cousins and I knew what the fish liked. We would bait our hooks and cast them out into the water. The key was to make sure the hook was invisible. I would try to wrap that bait around that hook any way I could to hide it. Satan's trick as he tries to tempt us is to deceive us and make the hook of sin invisible.

Satan knows what your flesh cries out for. But thank God, there is a difference between the weakness of the flesh and the power of the Spirit. Jesus' instructions about how we are to pray and commune with God are not instructions meant to produce simple prayers with no power. The type of prayer Jesus instructs us to pray is not a prayer that is recited only at bedtime. It is a prayer that becomes a catalyst into a life of prayer and recognizes that we need spiritual eyes to see and recognize the bait that satan is offering. We need spiritual eyes to see the vicious barb of sin that will destroy us once it has taken hold in our life.

My son, Will, loves to fish, and he's quite good at it. He and I went fishing a few years ago on a river near our home. Actually, Will was doing the fishing while I was sitting with him trying to read. There was a family fishing down the river a short distance from us, a father with a little boy and girl. When we learned to fish as children, we were instructed that too much noise would scare the fish away, so I learned to be quiet while fishing. But it seemed these children had not yet learned that lesson, so they were making a substantial amount of noise. That was fine, because I was enjoying my time with Will and watching these two little children fish. But the whole scene quickly changed.

The little boy reached back as far as he could to cast his line, and as he went into his forward-casting motion, he hooked his sister—in the face! Have you ever been hooked with a fishhook? I have, and let me assure you it will cause you to cry out in pain. The little girl let out a load scream. Since we were standing nearby, Will turned to me and whispered, "What should we do?" I didn't know what to do so all I could say was, "I don't know." Since the children's father was there, I thought it best to wait and see how he handled it rather than running over and getting in his way of trying to help.

Will and I watched as this father calmed down his little daughter and attempted to pull the fish hook out of her face. Somehow, by God's grace, the hook's barb did not go too far into her skin, so the father was able to easily pull the hook out of the little girl with surprisingly little incident. We were so relieved. Will continued to fish a little while longer once the scene calmed down, and I tried to continue reading and enjoying my time with Will.

When satan dangles his bait in front of us, it is always disguised as something appealing. The bait looks beautiful, it looks harmless, and it looks good. Satan knows what our flesh craves. But rarely do the hooks of satan come out as easily as that little girl's hook. Satan's hooks are vicious.

The prayer Jesus instructs us to pray, says, "Lord, I don't want to be led into temptation; help me to recognize the bait. I used to want this, but I want you to transform my desires so that I don't want what satan is offering." Satan is not going to offer what your spirit desires, but what the flesh desires. It is your flesh that needs to change! The only way you are going to recognize the bait from satan is when you are transformed by the power of the Holy Spirit. You have been given spiritual eyes to see what he is throwing your way.

James said we are "enticed" as we are led into sin. What looks good to you? There are certainly things that we, when living in sinfulness, will be tempted to do. The list of sins we are drawn to could be endless. We all have different weaknesses and fleshly desires. To be enticed means that we want what looks good to us. It means that we are affected by what we want or desire. This is where the prayer of transformation by the Spirit comes in. I am praying not only for the Lord to forgive me, not only for the Lord to heal me, but also for the Lord to transform my very nature and desires.

◇

Victory over sin can be experienced when the Holy Spirit transforms our desires. The truth is that we cannot be victorious over sin with willpower alone or with a simple desire to do right. No matter how strong we think we are, we cannot be victorious in our own strength. But when God renews our minds, when God transforms us by the power of the Holy Spirit, all that once enticed us to take the bait of sin will no longer look appetizing. Freedom is found when we allow God to transform our desires.

> *Victory over sin can be experienced*
> *when the Holy Spirit transforms our desires.*

Paul said it like this in Romans 8:1–3:

Therefore, there is now no condemnation for those who are in Christ Jesus, because through Christ Jesus the law of the Spirit who gives life has set you free from the law of sin and death. For what the law was powerless to do because it was weakened by the flesh, God did by sending his own Son in the likeness of sinful flesh to be a sin offering. And so he condemned sin in the flesh.

I've counseled Christian young people who were dating and in the process of looking for the spouse God had for them. They tell me of the battles against sexual temptation because they are dating and not yet married. They know that Scripture forbids sexual activity before marriage, but they were struggling with remaining pure during times of interaction. After hearing their stories, I realized that every time they failed in this manner, they had set themselves up for failure. They had placed themselves in situations and settings that enabled their failure by making it easy for them to give in to sexual temptation.

My advice would always be the same: If you're trying to win the victory over temptation, you are not going to win it in the back seat of a car or lying on a bed together. If you place yourself in a situation like that and then pray, "Oh God, give me grace to get out of this situation," often, you've already lost.

You're only going to win by having a lifestyle of prayer and letting God transform the desires of your heart. What we need is the power of the Holy Spirit that changes our desires so that what we used to want, we no longer want anymore. We need the power of the Holy Spirit to give us the wisdom to not be led into tempting situations. This comes through continual conversation with God.

STRENGTHENED:
A MOMENT OF FELLOWSHIP

I can do all this through him who gives me strength. (Philippians 4:13)

None of us, in our own strength, have any hope of living an abundant life free from sin's entrapment. It's only persistent, prevailing prayer that is our open doorway into righteous living and changing the desires of our heart. Pray with one or two other people, making this declaration of helplessness:

Lord, my power and strength are insufficient. I need you to change the desires of my heart and empower my freedom.

Pray this prayer of humility with other people. Believe together that Jesus is present, sufficient, and available to empower your life of Christlikeness.

That is life in the Spirit. That is not life according to the flesh. You are a miserable person if you are living according to the flesh while supposedly trying to please God, because you will fail over and over and over again. God wants to give you a life transformed by the Holy Spirit, enabling you to be victorious over sin. Paul continued in Romans 8:3–4:

> For what the law was powerless to do because it was weakened by the flesh, God did by sending his own Son in the likeness of sinful flesh to be a sin offering. And so he condemned sin in the flesh, in order that the righteous requirement of the law might be fully met in us, who do not live according to the flesh but according to the Spirit.

This spiritual transformation is not simply a decision that you make in a moment one day; it is a transformation that comes from the portals of heaven to change your desires and transform your love for self into a love for God and the will of God. We can be transformed through the Holy Spirit to have our desires changed and become hungrier for God than for the enticements of this world.

Jesus' instructions for a life of prayer run deeper than just words. He is instructing us in the Lord's Prayer to be transformed from the inside out, because, as James says, "Each person is tempted when they are dragged away." When the enemy puts the bait out there, if it's something you want, if it's something that looks good, and you take the bait that is hiding that hook, he will spiritually drag you away and reel you in.

This is not a game you are playing. This is a spiritual battle, and satan, like a roaring lion, is seeking whom he may devour. But Jesus Christ has made a way of escape for you. Sin does not seize you suddenly. As a Christian, if I am disobedient to God, the guilt and the shame wash over me, and I immediately realize this didn't happen in a mere moment. It was progressive. It was a slow process of giving into temptation time and time again. I gave way to more of the flesh and less of the Spirit.

Sin does not overtake you in an instant. Victory over sin is won through a life of prayer. You won't win in the moment of temptation if there has not been preparation through prayer. If your heart and desires have not been changed, there can be no true victory over sin.

Victory over sin is won in the prayer closet.
You won't win in the moment of temptation if there
has not been preparation through prayer.

Jesus deals with more than what we see on the outside; he deals with what is on the inside. The power of the Holy Spirit and the blood of Jesus Christ can transform our motives. We call it sanctification. Jesus makes you victorious through the Spirit.

If you're struggling, if you're battling temptation today, I cannot tell you every chain is going to be broken in an instant and that you will never struggle again. We have not only *been* sanctified, we are *being* sanctified, and we *will be* sanctified. This is a walk with God. Every day in this battle between the flesh and the Spirit, I want to give myself over to the Spirit rather than the flesh.

As we battle with sin, we have a cheerleader of sorts, though it goes much, much further than that. Hebrews 4:14–16 tells us:

> Therefore, since we have a great high priest who has ascended into heaven, Jesus the Son of God, let us hold firmly to the faith we profess. For we do not have a high priest who is unable to empathize with our weaknesses, but we have one who has been tempted in every way, just as we are—yet he did not sin. Let us then approach God's throne of grace with confidence, so that we may receive mercy and find grace to help us in our time of need.

Jesus will give us grace to help in our times of need. Hebrews 7:25 says it this way: "Therefore he is able to save completely those who come to God through him, because he always lives to intercede for them." As I am in this battle, as I am in this war against satan and against sin, there is a righteous Jesus Christ who sits at the right hand of the Father, making intercession for me and for you. And we can be victorious through him!

God offers you and me the greatest privilege we could imagine—the opportunity for conversation with him in the experience of prevailing prayer. A lifestyle of conversation with God, through speaking and listening to him, enables us to become like him. It is my prayer that you will respond to God's invitation for friendship with you and encounter his love and presence in your life.

FRIENDSHIP:
A MOMENT OF FELLOWSHIP

I pray that the eyes of your heart may be enlightened in order that you may know the hope to which he has called you. (Ephesians 1:18)

Claim the promise of Ephesians 1:18, that we might see and hear as Jesus does. Just as the Scripture notes that Abraham was a friend of God, rejoice together that you are also the friend of God and that he longs to reveal himself to you and involve you in his kingdom purposes. God wants to free you from sin, confide in you, and then co-labor with you for his eternal glory. Ask him to bless the fruitfulness of the work he has called you to do in this life of prevailing prayer.

Father, I want to complete the work you have for me. As I reflect on the privilege and the wonder of intimacy with you and co-laboring with you for eternal good, my heart is moved with _____. Continue to reveal yourself to me in prayer, as I impart your life and love to those I serve.

L4. *Rejoicing regularly in my identity as his beloved.*

Appendix 1

Corporate or Group Intercession

by Bill Eubank

ntercession is prayer that pleads with God for your needs and the needs of others. But it is also much more than that.

Intercession involves taking hold of God's will and refusing to let go until His will comes to pass. Intercessory prayer is not the same as prayers for yourself, or for "enlightenment," or for spiritual gifts, or for guidance, or any personal matter, or any glittering generality. Intercession is not just praying for someone else's needs. Intercession is praying with the real hope and real intent that God would step in and act for the positive advancement of some specific other person or groups of people or community. It is trusting God to act, even if it's not in the manner or timing we seek. God wants us to ask, even *urgently*. It is casting our weakness before God's strength, and (at its best) having a bit of God's' passion burn in us.

If you are born again, you are God's son or daughter (John 1:12). As His child, you have a direct "hotline" to God. At any time, you can boldly come into His presence (Hebrews 4:16). This incredible access to God is the basis for intercession. Once you are in God's presence, you can now discover His battle plan for the situation you are facing. Because prayer alone is not enough—you need a target for your prayers!

To discover God's plan, all you have to do is *ask*. The Bible says, "If any of you lacks wisdom, let him ask of God, who gives to all liberally and without reproach, and it will be given to him" (James 1:5). When we ask God for wisdom, His desires will become the focus of our prayers. Let God change the way you think. Then you will know how to do everything that is good and pleasing to Him (Romans 12:2).

In preparation to coming into a time of intercession, each person should individually pray and ask the Holy Spirit what He would have us pray. Here is some suggested prayer etiquette when interceding in a group:

1. Our prayers should be short and focused on the area that the Spirit is leading. Listen carefully to what your fellow intercessors are praying to see if the Spirit would have you add to or build on their prayer.

2. As we pray short focused prayers, it is easier for others to join us in agreement or add their prayer for similar needs.

3. Encourage others by agreeing or saying amen in a quiet voice when someone prays something with which your spirit bears witness.

4. There will be times when the Spirit will show a person Scripture that relates with what is being prayed. They can share the Scripture and connect what the Spirit is showing them.

5. Do not be afraid of silence as you pray. Every moment does not have to be filled with words. Sometimes the Lord causes the group to be silent, so that people have the time to clearly hear what the Spirit is saying to their hearts.

6. Group intercession is corporate in nature. The Holy Spirit will lead as He wills. Therefore, each participant should seek to sense what the Spirit would have him/her pray at any given time to contribute to the whole.

7. You may have a burning desire to pray in a certain direction, but it is important that you wait before the Spirit to make sure that He would have you offer prayer from your "burning desire."

8. There are times when the Spirit is not leading in the direction that you thought He was. This is where maturity reveals that it is our responsibility to sincerely seek His guidance and direction.

9. If a participant begins to share his/her thoughts with the group instead of speaking to God, the leader or person with discernment should gently encourage everyone to focus on God and speak directly to Him.

10. There will be time after corporate intercession to share ideas, thoughts, and experiences with each other.

11. The great blessing of effective corporate intercession should be a sense that that group has "heard" or understood the direction of the Spirit for that time and feel that they prayed in that way.

About the
Great Commandment Network

The Great Commandment Network is an international collaborative network of strategic kingdom leaders from the faith community, marketplace, education, and caregiving fields who prioritize the powerful simplicity of the words of Jesus to love God, love others, and see others become His followers (Matthew 22:37–40, Matthew 28:19–20).

THE GREAT COMMANDMENT NETWORK IS SERVED THROUGH THE FOLLOWING:

Relationship Press – This team collaborates, supports, and joins together with churches, denominational partners, and professional associates to develop, print, and produce resources that facilitate ongoing Great Commandment ministry.

The Center for Relational Leadership – Their mission is to teach, train, and mentor both ministry and corporate leaders in Great Commandment principles, seeking to equip leaders with relational skills so they might lead as Jesus led.

The Galatians 6:6 Retreat Ministry – This ministry offers a unique two-day retreat for ministers and their spouses for personal renewal and for reestablishing and affirming ministry and family priorities.

The Center for Relational Care (CRC) – The CRC provides therapy and support to relationships in crisis through an accelerated process of growth and healing, including Relational Care Intensives for couples, families, and singles.

For more information on how you, your church, ministry, denomination, or movement can be served by the Great Commandment Network write or call:

Great Commandment Network
2511 South Lakeline Blvd.
Cedar Park, Texas 78613
#800-881-8008

Or visit our website: www.GreatCommandment.net

A Spirit-Empowered Faith

Expresses Itself in Great Commission Living
Empowered by Great Commandment Love

 begins with the end in mind:
The Great Commission calls us
to make disciples.

"Go therefore and make disciples of all the nations, baptizing them in
the name of the Father and the Son and the Holy Spirit teaching them
to observe all things that I have commanded you; and lo, I am with
you always, even to the end of the age." (Matthew 28:19–20)

The ultimate goal of our faith journey is to relate to the person of Jesus, because it is our relational connection to Jesus that will produce Christ-likeness and spiritual growth. This relational perspective of discipleship is required if we hope to have a faith that is marked by the Spirit's power.

Models of discipleship that are based solely upon what we *know* and what we *do* are incomplete, lacking the empowerment of a life of loving and living intimately with Jesus. **A Spirit-empowered faith is relational and impossible to realize apart from a special work of the Spirit.** For example, the Spirit-empowered outcome of "listening to and hearing God" implies relationship—it is both relational in focus and requires the Holy Spirit's power to live.

 begins at the right place:
The Great Commandment calls us to
start with loving God and loving others.

"'You shall love the Lord your God with all your heart, with all your soul,
and with all your mind.' This is the first and great commandment.
And the second is like it: 'You shall love your neighbor as yourself.'
On these two commandments hang all the Law and the Prophets."

(Matthew 22:37–40)

Relevant discipleship does not begin with doctrines or teaching, parables or stewardship—but with loving the Lord with all your heart, mind, soul, and strength and then loving the people closest to you. Since Matthew 22:37–40 gives us the first and greatest commandment, *a Spirit-empowered faith starts where the Great Commandment tells us to start: A disciple must first learn to deeply love the Lord and to express His love to the "nearest ones"—his or her family, church, and community (and in that order).*

 embraces a relational process of Christlikeness.

Scripture reminds us that there are three sources of light for our journey: Jesus, His Word, and His people. The process of discipleship (or becoming more like Jesus) occurs as we relate intimately with each source of light.

"Walk while you have the light, lest darkness overtake you." (John 12:35)

Spirit-empowered discipleship will require a lifestyle of:
- Fresh encounters with Jesus (John 8:12)
- Frequent experiences of Scripture (Psalm 119:105)
- Faithful engagement with God's people (Matthew 5:14)

 can be defined with observable outcomes using a biblical framework.

The metrics for measuring Spirit-empowered faith or the growth of a disciple come from Scripture and are organized/framed around four distinct dimensions of a disciple who serves.

And He Himself gave some to be apostles, some prophets,
some evangelists, and some pastors and teachers,
for the equipping of the saints for the work of ministry,
for the edifying of the body of Christ.
(Ephesians 4:11–12)

A relational framework for organizing Spirit-Empowered Discipleship Outcomes draws from a cluster analysis of several Greek (*diakoneo, leitourgeo, douleuo*) and Hebrew words ('*abad, Sharat*), which elaborate on the Ephesians 4:12 declaration that Christ's followers are to be equipped for works of ministry or service. Therefore, the 40 Spirit-Empowered Faith Outcomes have been identified and organized around:

- Serving/loving the Lord – *While they were **ministering** to the Lord and fasting* (Acts 13:2 NASB).[1]
- Serving/loving the Word – *But we will devote ourselves to prayer and to the **ministry** of the word* (Acts 6:4 NASB).[2]
- Serving/loving people – *Through love **serve** one another* (Galatians 5:13 NASB).[3]
- Serving/loving His mission – *Now all these things are from God, who reconciled us to Himself through Christ and gave us the **ministry** of reconciliation* (2 Corinthians 5:18 NASB).[4]

---

1 Ferguson, David L. *Great Commandment Principle*. Cedar Park, Texas: Relationship Press, 2013.

2 Ferguson, David L. *Relational Foundations*. Cedar Park, Texas: Relationship Press, 2004.

3 Ferguson, David L. *Relational Discipleship*. Cedar Park, Texas: Relationship Press, 2005.

4 "Spirit Empowered Outcomes," www.empowered21.com, Empowered 21 Global Council, http://empowered21.com/discipleship-materials/.

A Spirit-Empowered Disciple

 ## A SPIRIT-EMPOWERED DISCIPLE LOVES THE LORD THROUGH

L1. Practicing thanksgiving in all things
Enter into His gates with thanksgiving (Ps. 100:4). *In everything give thanks* (1 Th. 5:18). *As sorrowful, yet always rejoicing* (2 Cor. 6:10).

L2. Listening to and hearing God for direction and discernment
"Speak, Lord, for Your servant hears" (1 Sam. 3:8–9). *Mary, who also sat at Jesus' feet and heard His word* (Lk. 10:38–42). *And the Lord said, "Shall I hide from Abraham what I am doing … ?"* (Gen. 18:17). *But as the same anointing teaches you concerning all things …* (1 Jn. 2:27).

L3. Experiencing God as He really is through deepened intimacy with Him
"Hear, O Israel: The Lord our God, the Lord is one! You shall love the Lord your God with all your heart, with all your soul, and with all your strength" (Deut. 6:4–5). *Therefore the Lord will wait, that He may be gracious to you; and therefore He will be exalted, that He may have mercy on you. For the Lord is a God of justice …* (Is. 30:18). See also John 14:9.

L4. Rejoicing regularly in my identity as "His Beloved"
And his banner over me was love (Song of Sol. 2:4). *To the praise of the glory of His grace, by which He made us accepted in the Beloved* (Eph. 1:6). *For so He gives His beloved sleep* (Ps. 127:2).

L5. Living with a passionate longing for purity and to please Him in all things
Who may ascend into the hill of the Lord? … He who has clean hands and a pure heart (Ps. 24:3–4). *Beloved, let us cleanse ourselves from all filthiness of flesh and spirit, perfecting holiness in the fear of God* (2 Cor. 7:1). *"I always do those things that please Him"* (Jn. 8:29). *"Though He slay me, yet will I trust Him"* (Job 13:15).

L6.   Consistent practice of self-denial, fasting, and solitude rest
He turned and said to Peter, "Get behind me, Satan! You are offense to Me, for you are not mindful of the things of God, but the things of men" (Mt. 16:23). "But you, when you fast …" (Mt. 6:17). "Be still, and know that I am God" (Ps. 46:10).

L7.   Entering often into Spirit-led praise and worship
Bless the Lord, O my soul, and all that is within me (Ps. 103:1). Serve the Lord with fear (Ps. 2:11). I thank You, Father, Lord of heaven and earth (Mt. 11:25).

L8.   Disciplined, bold, and believing prayer
Praying always with all prayer and supplication in the Spirit (Eph. 6:18). "Call to Me, and I will answer you" (Jer. 33:3). If we ask anything according to His will, He hears us. And if we know that He hears us, whatever we ask, we know that we have the petitions that we have asked of Him (1 Jn. 5:14–15).

L9.   Yielding to the Spirit's fullness as life in the Spirit brings supernatural intimacy with the Lord, manifestation of divine gifts, and witness of the fruit of the Spirit
For by one Spirit we were all baptized into one body—whether Jews or Greeks, whether slaves or free—and have all been made to drink into one Spirit (1 Cor. 12:13). "But you shall receive power when the Holy Spirit has come upon you" (Acts 1:8). But the manifestation of the Spirit is given to each one for the profit of all (1 Cor. 12:7). See also 1 Pet. 4:10 and Rom. 12:6.

L10.   Practicing the presence of the Lord, yielding to the Spirit's work of Christlikeness
But we all, with unveiled face, … are being transformed into the same from glory to glory, just as by the Spirit of the Lord (2 Cor. 3:18). As the deer pants for the water brooks, so pants my soul after You, O God (Ps. 42:1).

A SPIRIT-EMPOWERED DISCIPLE LIVES THE WORD THROUGH

W1. Frequently being led by the Spirit into deeper love for the One who wrote the Word

" 'You shall love the Lord your God … .' 'You shall love neighbor as yourself.' On these two commandments hang all the Law and the Prophets" (Mt. 22:37–40). *And I will delight myself in Your commandments, which I love.* (Ps. 119:47). *"The fear of the LORD is clean … . More to be desired are they than gold … sweeter also than honey"* (Ps. 19:9–10).

W2. Being a "living epistle" in reverence and awe as His Word becomes real in my life, vocation, and calling

You are our epistle written in our hearts, known and read by all men (2 Cor. 3:2). *And the Word became flesh and dwelt among us* (Jn. 1:14). *Husbands, love your wives … cleanse her with the washing of water by the word* (Eph. 5:25–26). *See also Tit. 2:5. And whatever you do, do it heartily, as to the Lord and not to men* (Col. 3:23).

W3. Yielding to the Scripture's protective cautions and transforming power to bring life change in me

Through Your precepts I get understanding; therefore I hate every false way (Ps. 119:104). *"Let it be to me according to your word"* (Lk. 1:38). *How can a young man cleanse his way? By taking heed according to Your word* (Ps. 119:9). See also Col. 3:16–17.

W4. Humbly and vulnerably sharing of the Spirit's transforming work through the Word

I will speak of your testimonies also before kings, and will not be ashamed (Ps. 119:46). *Preach the word! Be ready in season and out of season* (2 Tim. 4:2).

W5. Meditating consistently on more and more of the Word hidden in the heart

Your word I have hidden in my heart, that I might not sin against You (Ps. 119:11). *Let the words of my mouth and the meditation of my heart be acceptable in Your sight, O Lord, my strength and my Redeemer* (Ps. 19:14).

W6. Encountering Jesus in the Word for deepened transformation in Christlikeness

But we all, with unveiled face, … are being transformed into the same image from glory to glory, just as by the Spirit of the Lord (2 Cor. 3:18). *If you abide in Me, and My words abide in you, you will ask what you desire, and it shall be done for you* (Jn. 15:7). See also Lk. 24:32, Ps. 119:136, and 2 Cor. 1:20.

W7. A life explained as one of "experiencing Scripture"

But this is what was spoken by the prophet Joel (Acts 2:16). *This is my comfort in my affliction, for Your word has given me life* (Ps. 119:50). *My soul breaks with longing for Your judgements at all times* (Ps. 119:20).

W8. Living "naturally supernatural" in all of life as His Spirit makes the written Word (*logos*) the living Word (rhema)

*So then aith comes by hearing, and hearing by the word (*rhema*) of God* (Rom. 10:17). *Your word is a lamp to my feet and a light to my path* (Ps. 119:105).

W9. Living abundantly "in the present" as His Word brings healing to hurt and anger, guilt, fear, and condemnation—which are heart hindrances to life abundant

"The thief does not come except to steal, and to kill, and to destroy" (Jn. 10:10). *I will run the course of Your commandments, for You shall enlarge my heart* (Ps. 119:32). *"And you shall know the truth, and the truth shall make you free"* (Jn. 8:32). *Stand fast therefore in the liberty by which Christ has made us free, and do not be entangled again with a yoke of bondage* (Gal. 5:1).

W10.   Implicit, unwavering trust that His Word will never fail
"The grass withers, the flower fades, but the word of our God stands forever" (Is. 40:8). *"So shall My word be that goes forth from My mouth; it shall not return to Me void"* (Is. 55:11).

A SPIRIT-EMPOWERED DISCIPLE LOVES PEOPLE THROUGH

P1.   Living a Spirit-led life of doing good in all of life: relationships and vocation, community and calling
Who went about doing good … (Acts 10:38). *"Let your light so shine before men, that they may see your good works and glorify your Father in heaven"* (Mt. 5:16). *"But love your enemies, do good, and lend, hoping for nothing in return; and your reward will be great, and you will be sons of the Most High. For He is kind to the unthankful and evil"* (Lk. 6:35). See also Rom. 15:2.

P2.   "Startling people" with loving initiatives to "give first"
"Give, and it will be given to you: good measure, pressed down, shaken together, and running over will be put into your bosom" (Lk. 6:38). *Then Jesus said, "Father, forgive them, for they do not know what they do"* (Lk. 23:34). See also Lk. 23:43 and Jn. 19:27.

P3.   Discerning the relational needs of others with a heart to give of His love
Let no corrupt word proceed out of your mouth, but what is good for necessary edification, that it might impart grace to the hearers (Eph. 4:29). *And my God shall supply all your need according to His riches in glory by Christ Jesus* (Phil. 4:19). See also Lk. 6:30.

P4. Seeing people as needing BOTH redemption from sin AND intimacy in relationships, addressing both human fallen-ness and aloneness

But God demonstrates His own love toward us, in that while we were still sinners, Christ died for us (Rom. 5:8). *And when Jesus came to the place, He looked up and saw him, and said to him, "Zacchaeus, make haste and come down, for today I must stay at your house"* (Lk. 19:5). See also Mk. 8:24 and Gen. 2:18.

P5. Ministering His life and love to our nearest ones at home and with family as well as faithful engagement in His body, the church

Husbands, likewise, dwell with them with understanding, giving honor to the wife, as to the weaker vessel, and as being heirs together of the grace of life, that your prayers may not be hindered (1 Pet. 3:7). See also 1 Pet. 3:1 and Ps. 127:3.

P6. Expressing the fruit of the Spirit as a lifestyle and identity

But the fruit of the Spirit is love, joy, peace, longsuffering, kindness, goodness, faithfulness, gentleness, self-control (Gal. 5:22–23). *A man's stomach shall be satisfied from the fruit of his mouth; From the produce of his lips he shall be filled* (Prov. 18:20).

P7. Expecting and demonstrating the supernatural as His spiritual gifts are made manifest and His grace is at work by His Spirit

In mighty signs and wonders, by the power of the Spirit of God, so that from Jerusalem and round about to Illyricum I have fully preached the gospel of Christ (Rom. 15:19). *"Most assuredly, I say to you, he who believes in Me, the works that I do he will do also"* (Jn. 14:12). See also 1 Cor. 14:1.

P8. Taking courageous initiative as a peacemaker, reconciling relationships along life's journey

Be at peace among yourselves (1 Th. 5:13). *For He Himself is our peace, who has made both one, and has broken down the middle wall of separation* (Eph. 2:14). *Confess your trespasses to one another, and pray for one another, that you may be healed* (Jas. 5:16).

P9. Demonstrating His love to an ever growing network of "others" as He continues to challenge us to love "beyond our comfort"

He who says, "I know Him," and does not keep His commandments, is a liar, and the truth is not in him (1 Jn. 2:4). *If someone says, "I love God," and hates his brother, he is a liar; for he who does not love his brother whom he has seen, how can he love God whom he has not seen?* (1 Jn. 4:20).

P10. Humbly acknowledging to the Lord, ourselves, and others that it is Jesus in and through us who is loving others at their point of need

"Take My yoke upon you and learn from Me, for I am gentle and lowly in heart, and you will find rest for your souls" (Mt. 11:29). *"If I then, your Lord and Teacher, have washed your feet, you also ought to wash one another's feet"* (Jn. 13:14).

A SPIRIT-EMPOWERED DISCIPLE LIVES HIS MISSION THROUGH

M1. Imparting the gospel and one's very life in daily activities and relationships, vocation and community

So, affectionately longing for you, we were well pleased to impart to you not only the gospel of God, but also our own lives, because you had become dear to us (1 Th. 2:8–9). See also Eph. 6:19.

M2. Expressing and extending the kingdom of God as compassion, |justice, love, and forgiveness are shared

"I must preach the kingdom of God to the other cities also, because for this purpose I have been sent" (Lk. 4:43). *"As You sent Me into the world, I also have sent them into the world"* (Jn. 17:18). *Restore to me the joy of Your salvation, and uphold me by Your generous Spirit. Then I will teach transgressors Your ways, and sinners shall be converted to You* (Ps. 51:12–13). See also Mic. 6:8.

M3. Championing Jesus as the only hope of eternal life and abundant living

"Nor is there salvation in any other, for there is no other name under heaven given among men by which we must be saved" (Acts 4:12). *"The thief does not come except to steal, and to kill, and to destroy. I have come so that they may have life, and that they have it more abundantly"* (Jn. 10:10). See also Acts 4:12 and Jn. 14:6.

M4. Yielding to the Spirit's role to convict others as He chooses, resisting expressions of condemnation

"And when He has come, He will convict the world of sin, and of righteousness, and of judgment" (Jn. 16:8). *Who is he who condemns? It is Christ who died, and furthermore is also risen, who is even at the right hand of God, who also makes intercession for us* (Rom. 8:34). See also Rom. 8:1.

M5. Ministering His life and love to the "least of these"

"Then He will answer them saying, 'Assuredly, I say to you inasmuch as you did not do it to one of the least of these, you did not do it to Me' " (Mt. 25:45). *Pure and undefiled religion before God and the Father is this: to visit orphans and widows in their trouble, and to keep oneself unspotted from the world* (Jas. 1:27).

M6.   Bearing witness of a confident peace and expectant hope in God's lordship in all things

Now may the Lord of peace Himself give you peace always in every way. The Lord be with you all (2 Thess. 3:16). *And let the peace of God rule in your hearts, to which also you were called in one body; and be thankful* (Col. 3:15). See also Rom. 8:28 and Ps. 146:5.

M7.   Faithfully sharing of time, talent, gifts, and resources in furthering His mission

Of which I became a minister according to the stewardship from God which was given to me for you, to fulfill the word of God (Col. 1:25). *"For everyone to whom much is given, from him much will be required"* (Lk. 12:48). See also 1 Cor. 4:1–2.

M8.   Attentive listening to others' story, vulnerably sharing of our story, and a sensitive witness of Jesus' story as life's ultimate hope; developing your story of prodigal, preoccupied and pain-filled living; listening for others' story and sharing Jesus' story

But sanctify the Lord God in your hearts, and always be ready to give a defense to everyone who asks you a reason for the hope that is in you, with meekness and fear (1 Pet. 3:15). *"For this my son was dead and is alive again"* (Luke 15:24). See also Mk. 5:21–42 and Jn. 9:1–35.

M9.   Pouring our life into others, making disciples who in turn make disciples of others

"Go therefore and make disciples of all the nations, baptizing them in the name of the Father and of the Son and of the Holy Spirit, teaching them to observe all things that I commanded you; and lo, I am with you always, even to the end of the age" (Mt. 28:19–20). See also 2 Tim. 2:2.

M10. Living submissively within His body, the Church, as instruction and encouragement; reproof and correction are graciously received by faithful disciples

Submitting to one another in the fear of God (Eph. 5:21). *Brethren, if a man is overtaken in any trespass, you who are spiritual restore such a one in a spirit of gentleness, considering yourself lest you also be tempted* (Gal. 6:1). See also Gal. 6:2.

Acknowledgments

Thank you to my wife, Renee. You are my sunshine! I love you, and I am thankful God gave you to me as a gift. Your selfless life is always an inspiration to me. Every day with you is my favorite day.

Thank you, Will, Tayler, and Chris. Renee and I are blessed with the greatest children and son-in-law we could have ever imagined. You are all we have prayed for. Thank you for always giving the encouragement to follow God's will for our family.

Thank you to Marsha Robinson who has spent countless hours on this project. Without your creativity and talent this would have been impossible.

Thank you to my friend, Dr. David Ferguson, and the Great Commandment Network team for your wonderful contribution to *Conversation with God*. Your heart of serving with excellence blesses the kingdom of God every day.

Thank you to the BroadStreet Publishing team. You are all such a joy to work with. I have constantly felt the hand of God as we have put this project together. May the name of Jesus be lifted up in all we have done!

Lastly, I am thankful for the heritage in my family of praying women. Both my grandmothers, Beatrice Sutton and Ruby Griffus, were tremendous women of faith and prayer. This heritage of prayer lives on in my mother, Janette Sutton. She spends more time in conversation with God than any person I have ever known. Because of her prayers, I was able to marry a woman like Renee, who also knows how to pray mightily.

May my mother's words be fulfilled in us: "Go with a prayer on your heart daily, and be not far from it."

About the Author

Brian Sutton serves as the executive director of discipleship and leadership development for the Church of God of Prophecy, a leading Christian movement serving in 135 nations. After having ministered as a senior pastor for twenty-five years, most recently serving as lead pastor of the Peerless Road Church, he accepted his current role to facilitate the spiritual and professional development of the ministry of the Church of God of Prophecy and develop Christian discipleship processes for the movement. Additionally, he serves as the publisher of the denomination's official magazine, *The White Wing Messenger*, and as a member of the movement's corporate board of directors, a position he has held since 2010. He also serves as a member of the Pentecostal/Charismatic Churches of North America Discipleship Commission.

Brian has earned a Bachelor of Science Degree in Organizational Management from Covenant College in Lookout Mountain, Georgia; a Master of Arts degree in Church Ministries from Pentecostal Theological Seminary in Cleveland, Tennessee; and a Master of Arts Degree in Religion from Gordon-Conwell Theological Seminary in Boston, Massachusetts. He is currently pursuing his Doctor of Ministry degree in Global Pentecostalism from Gordon-Conwell Theological Seminary.

He and his wife, Renee (a breast cancer survivor), have been married since 1990. They have a son (Will), a daughter (Tayler), and son-in-law (Chris). The family resides in Cleveland, Tennessee.